HARNESSING YOUR ADULT ADHD SUPERPOWERS

Holistic Lifestyle Solutions to Transform Your Productivity, Focus, and Well-Being

M. Yvette Quintana

For my intelligent, gorgeous, creative, happy, loving, and soulful daughter, Paisley. Thank you for your unique energy & radiant light that you bring to this world.

Medical Disclaimer

AUTHOR'S DISCLAIMER

FREE E-Books!

Sign up to get these
valuable- downloadable
e-book gifts:

Goal Setting
ADHD Workbook

Anti -Inflammatory
Cookbook

or type in: https://crafty-artist-5616.ck.page/b11efc1a00

Contents

Introduction   xi
Reframing Your Mindset   xiii
Defining ADHD   xxiii
Understanding ADHD & Transforming It Into
Your Superpower   xxv

Part One
THE BODY

1. A Healthy Diet To Thrive   3
2. Consistent Exercise For Mental Clarity   25
3. The Power Of Sleep   37

Part Two
THE MIND

4. The Modern Mind   51
5. Structuring Your Days   64
6. Structuring Your Environment   74

Part Three
THE SPIRIT

7. Breathing & Meditation   85
8. Hypnosis, Visualization & Affirmations   99
9. Mindfulness Training   109
10. Creativity: The Ultimate Advantage of ADHD   119

Conclusion   129
Endnotes   133
Bibliography   143
Afterword   149
About the Author   151

Introduction

Reframing Your Mindset

"Why fit in when you were born to stand out?"
- Dr. Suess

Heroes come in many different shapes, colors, talents, and powers. But when we think of a hero, what comes to mind? Maybe it's an image of someone who has their life together and can manage two different worlds while simultaneously saving the world. It's a lot to juggle. After all, superheroes have to hide their private lives while handling their superhero side, being responsible, and accomplishing impossible feats.

If you think about it, people with Attention Deficit Hyperactivity Disorder (ADHD) are very much like these super-heroes, hiding their "true selves" under a mask they show the world, masking who they are. You might think the similarities end there. In reality, many symptoms of ADHD can be reframed to become something empowering. Dare I say it; they may even become *superpowers*.

As an adult, I suspected that I had attention deficit disorder. I called it my 'AADD'- adult attention deficit disorder. Like many people with ADHD, I turned to sports as an outlet for my energy and extreme enthusiasm. I had the great fortune to grow up in the mountains of Utah, which led me to find running, biking, and skiing as a way to channel my abundant energy. Sports, undoubtedly, set me on a positive path in life.

Later in life, I joked about my AADD, trying to cover for my constant interruptions in conversations. People would point it out, calling me rude, and I would get my feelings hurt. Hey, I thought, wasn't I just adding witty banter to a laborious conversation!?!? The bubble over my cartoon head would read– "Let"s move this conversation along. Don't you see, I need to get going?!"

Despite my impatience, I genuinely worked on controlling my squirrel impulses to blurt out snazzy antidotes and advice to friends. I used to beat myself up over it, going over conversations in my mind at night.

Ultimately, after years of living in my head— I realize that I am a loving, energetic, compassionate, humorous extrovert who happens to talk too much, interrupt, bounce around and lose my phone–A LOT. Squirrel is my power animal, and I'm proud to have so much energy in this life that propels me to adventure. If you get to choose the Pooh character you are most like, I am 70% Tigger. I also have the compassion, happiness and worry of Kanga, Pooh and Rabbit.

With the help of this book, you can learn to take control of your ADHD symptoms and how to use the better parts of ADHD to your advantage. Do you desire to edit videos and create art? Do you need to be outside? Think about guiding people on hiking tours or fly fishing. Alternatively, you could teach music in your community. These are some of the many superpower careers where people with ADHD can contribute fabulously!

In the past few decades, ADHD has become less of a disorder that requires fixing or curing. It's become more of a personal characteristic that can be a curse if left to its own device or a gift if managed and harnessed.

Adult ADHD essentially goes unnoticed. As many as 75 % of adults that may have ADHD don't *know it*, according to New York University psychiatrist Len Adler.[1]

A child may be assessed for ADHD but may not meet the threshold and get sidelined. Individuals who can get by without a diagnosis in childhood may later develop into unseen adult ADHD and wonder the entire time, "What is wrong with me?"

While hyperactivity is a common ADHD symptom seen outwardly in children, adults tend to appear more inattentive. Adult hyperactivity may manifest internally through stress and anxiety. You might always feel restless, unable to sit still, struggle with avoiding interrupting others, and feel like your brain is never-ending chatter. Inattentiveness can show up in work and home life, with a pattern of losing everyday items, being incredibly forgetful, not keeping up with the details, and feeling disorganized and all over the place.

Do you ever find yourself doing lots of tasks simultaneously to feel productive before realizing you haven't done much of anything? Well, that *may* be an ADHD symptom.

Mild adult ADHD can display as impulsivity, leading to risky behavior and overspending — acts that adults often write off as bad habits. However, this behavior can be compulsive and hard to dismantle if you don't know the root cause.

Even worse, overlooking your ADHD long enough can lead to low self-esteem, feeling like you are always behind or that you are a failure. It can cause issues in your career, preventing you from meeting your long-term goals. Both platonic and romantic relationships may suffer due to forgetfulness and concentration issues. You may be at higher risk for mood disorders, anxiety, depression, losing your drive and joy in life, and even substance abuse.

People with ADHD are great at "masking," just like our comic book superheroes. "Masking" describes behaving "normally" by adopting the traits of people around you who seem to know what they're doing. We're good at acting focused and on track, even when our brain feels like it's going on a rollercoaster. Unfortunately, masking can only go so far. Eventually, you might find yourself stuck, burnt out, and lacking motivation. Jobs and relationships may suffer due to a lack of concentration, mood swings, boredom, and sudden irritability. All of this, without explanation, can push your self-concept and confidence downhill.

I was undiagnosed for a long time and suffered until I faced it in my fifties. I realized how little I knew about ADHD except for common knowledge that tended to be oversimplified.

Our daughter suffered from ADHD in grade school. In college, it developed into anxiety and stress. Noting our similarities, I got my own diagnosis, which was mostly ADD. I wondered how my milder symptoms compared to hers and how I could help her? As a result, I went into the hyper-focus mode, researching ADHD, and examined how the three main pillars of health; body, mind, and spirit are connected. I wanted to examine how a healthy lifestyle has helped me to control my ADHD, resulting in milder symptoms.

This book is the result and outlines holistic lifestyle changes that can greatly help improve ADHD symptoms. We can all agree there is no cure for ADHD, but healthy lifestyle changes can greatly improve the quality of life. You may also find that some of your symptoms can be reframed and become your super-power, like energy for sports and creativity for amazing artistic endeavors.

I look to the people in my life that have harnessed their ADHD superpowers for a positive outcome. ADHD friends with phenomenal creative skills and athletes that have accomplished far-out goals and adventures, have all been my heroes and inspiration.

Earlier in life, I struggled with harnessing my ADD superpowers. Being an extrovert, I was often distracted by shiny object syndrome and a 'fear of missing out' (FOMO). I was constantly chasing my tail all over town, searching for dopamine highs from socialization, shopping, or exercise (luckily). I now understand how to harness my energy for the better. In fact, I learned many lessons from the period of the Covid lockdown, where I was forced to stay put, and be more reflexive and productive on my own terms.

If you're like me, you may go through life unaware you have a problem. Maybe you thought *you* were the problem. No matter the case, I'm here to tell you that you're not alone. Whether you are just dipping your toes into the subject, you are suspicious that you may have ADHD or were recently diagnosed, the strategies in this book can help you. You want to understand yourself and use tools to help you become more successful and productive. The good news is that ADHD can give you that energy.

Most people think of ADHD on a binary scale. Either you have it, or you don't. Think of it as more of a spectrum that us ADHD folk all fall somewhere on. Some may especially struggle with impulsivity, and others with emotional regulation. ADHD has several subtypes that can appear differently depending on age, gender, and context: inattentive type, hyperactive-impulsive type, and a combination of both. ADHD is far from our preconceptions, making it harder to detect earlier.

The good news? Having ADHD isn't a death sentence. It doesn't make you less capable than anyone else of living to the fullest. By understanding your individual needs, you can address them adequately. If you are unsure if you have ADHD, get a concrete diagnosis with a professional evaluation. From there, you can make more informed decisions.

This book is not meant to replace professional medical advice. Still, it can help as some advice to push you towards improving your life if you think you may have undiagnosed ADHD or identify with any significant ADHD symptoms. I wanted to make an accessible guide that could resonate with people who deal with these symptoms, regardless of being diagnosed or not. I bet nearly everyone suffers from one of these things or another, and many of the tips I will give you are things that can change your life for the better. A holistic lifestyle is the foundation for health and can maximize your talents regardless of your place on the ADHD spectrum.

You'll find many tips here: lifestyle shifts that seem simple to implement. You'll find yourself saying at times: "What? That's it? That's all I need to do?" And yes, sometimes, it is! Some of the best hacks are straightforward, but when done consistently, they can lead to amazing long-term benefits to your concentration and productivity. It can take discipline, self-love, and patience, but implementing a few of these habits every week can lead you on the path to becoming your own superhero.

It is a matter of taking personal responsibility for your well-being. By implementing holistic management, you can harness ADHD just like the many people who have been able to achieve success despite it. Famous people like Olympian Michael Phelps, singer Justin Timberlake, and notable actors Emma Watson and Johnny Depp all have ADHD. Their achievement is proof that this condition does not have to limit us. ADHD may be a deficit of attention, but some of the most creative, intelligent, and productive people overcome it. We can do remarkable feats when our energy is channeled in the right direction.

ADHD CAN MAKE US...

Hyper-Focused: When it comes to our passions, we can have intense periods of concentration ("the zone") in which the world around us disappears until the task is complete.

Highly energized: We can have exhilarating bursts of energy that we can direct into life, art, work, or athletics.

Spontaneous: Impulsivity isn't always negative. It can allow us to be open to new adventures, experiences, and excitement in life.

Creative: Our overstimulated brains can make non-linear connections others can't. It can give us a fresh outlook, an inventive method for a task, or allow us to tap into our right brains to create beautiful things.

Humorous: We are wired for quirky, witty and hilarious —who doesn't need more laughter in their life?!

How we frame situations is so powerful. Two people with the same problem can travel along *very* different trajectories. One might see the struggle as a burden, while another might see it as an opportunity for growth. It's all about reframing, a concept used in some of the most successful psychotherapeutic treatments.

All the "NEGATIVE" aspects of ADHD are only limiting when considered through a neurotypical context. By "neurotypical," I mean the state of having a brain and neurological anatomy that is developed and operating as functionally as possible, as is the average. When you look past this neurotypical lens, you can have an open-minded and positive understanding of ADHD.

The way you look at something always affects how you approach it. If you want to manage ADHD and use it to your advantage, you must see it in as positive of a light as possible to open your mind to your hidden gifts.

Medication can definitely be a helpful solution. Ideally, though, you want to use it as a way to tame more severe symptoms, freeing you to focus on improving some of your self-destructive habits. Clinicians will recommend meds alongside behavioral-based treatment because certain lifestyles can exacerbate ADHD symptoms. A healthy mind, a healthy body, and a healthy soul are the keys to gaining mastery over your ADHD.

Managing ADHD holistically means taking all facets of life and health into account. In this book, we are going to tackle ADHD through three essential facets –Body, Mind, and Spirit.

1. **Body**: Physical health impacts both brain and mental health. A healthy diet, exercise, and sleep habits create a stronger foundation to manage the more problematic ADHD symptoms

2. **Mind:** ADHD starts in the brain. You can utilize behavioral habits to manage the neurotransmitters involved in ADHD symptoms, like goal setting, time management, and organization.

3. **Spirit**: Last but not least, your soul also needs nourishment. Fight against mental health concerns with techniques like deep breathing, mindfulness, self-hypnosis, journaling, self-love, and compassion.

To be clear, I am not a medical professional, and this book does not serve to diagnose or treat. I am just a simple gal with ADHD, with other members of my family also facing degrees of ADHD. I have been where you are, feeling confused and hopeless at times. Realizing I had ADHD freed me because I could pinpoint areas of my life that needed improvement and *how* to target them. I want to help you do the same.

Having an official ADHD diagnosis is not a requirement to benefit from the holistic techniques in this guide. If you identify any challenging signs and symptoms we'll discuss, these strategies can help turn your life around.

A NOTE ON HOW TO USE THIS BOOK:

You may want to read sections of the book that interest you first. Not a problem, skip around— pick and choose what resonates with you. Make small changes in your life and build as you feel inspired. Don't try to make massive changes all at once, only to become overwhelmed and frustrated. Love yourself by making slow and steady progress to improve your health and well-being.

Become your own hero! You can do it—let's dive in!

Defining ADHD

Understanding ADHD & Transforming It Into Your Superpower

One of the most profound truths I've learned is this: *you fear what you don't know.* What is the antidote to fear of the unknown? Learning about it.

Upon discovering they have ADHD, many people feel scared or worried about what life may look like. Other adults spend most of their lives avoiding a diagnosis, pretending they are okay; they may think that all they need is more grit to work harder and be like everyone else.

I felt the same way and didn't understand why I was so anxious. Time was never my friend, and felt I was constantly battling getting even small things accomplished. Even when suspicions entered my mind that I may have ADHD, I brushed it off and pushed myself harder.

The diagnosis itself may relieve some people, but for others, it feels like everything they have ever known in their life has changed. It's undoubtedly a scary thing, especially going into it when our preconceptions about ADHD. We may think it solidifies a truth within us that we are permanently different or damaged. However, you can dissolve that fear by learning more about the multifaceted disorder that can manifest in various ways.

Understanding and accepting ADHD is the perfect first step in searching for your superpowers, regardless of your diagnosis. This journey step is about reframing the classic ADHD characteristics into empowering qualities to step into your superhero self. This chapter will clarify some key ADHD signs, especially ones you suspect are keeping you from reaching your goals.

UNDERSTANDING ADHD

You may already be familiar with ADHD, but let's break down what it is at its core. First, here's what ADHD is NOT: a mental illness, or a behavioral disorder solely caused by the overconsumption of technology and games.

ADHD is actually a hereditary, brain-based developmental disorder — it is neurological, which means specific parts of the brain were not fully or adequately developed. Those parts of the brain are primarily a part of the brain's self-management system. If the system is out of whack, it can lead to three presentations of ADHD: inattentive, in which there is difficulty managing one's focus; hyperactive, in which it's challenging to manage one's energy, impulses, and emotions; or combined, which is self-explanatory.

It is impossible to 'get' ADHD by simply having poor attention and time management habits. However, if you have ADHD, you can improve it by building skills related to executive functioning.

Executive function is a critical part of our brain that encompasses some of the essential self-regulation aspects. In other words, it powers our self-control and ability to adapt to situations. We use executive functioning to drive our working memory, which is our short-term memory. It enables us to weigh the risks and rewards of a potential action and make decisions from that. Finally, it gives us the mental flexibility to adapt to various situations, like quickly flipping attention between many different things or taking in more than a few pieces of information simultaneously.[2]

In summary, executive functioning covers these facets:

1. Control over actions and reactions
   2. Understanding and following instruction
   3. Working memory
   4. Processing emotions
   5. Learning from errors
   6. Making decisions
   7. Mental flexibility

As you can see, executive function is one of the key things that sets humans apart from animals. It offers a barrier between our impulses and our higher self, promoting healthy, fulfilling behavior.

What's the relationship between executive functioning and ADHD? Well, just based on the abilities that executive functioning gives us, it's evident that the two are closely intertwined. With ADHD, we see poor self-control when it comes to impulsive behavior, difficulty with regulating emotions, and difficulty with focusing, planning, and carrying out tasks. ADHD brains try to multi-task but have difficulty absorbing too many stimuli simultaneously. In this way, ADHD is an executive functioning deficit disorder.

On the bright side, nearly all the aspects involved in executive functioning are buildable skills. We all have the capacity for them, no matter where we start or how severe our symptoms are.

COMMON SIGNS AND SYMPTOMS

The media has oversimplified ADHD as a condition marked by being incredibly forgetful, distracted, and ridiculously energetic. Some of this is valid. Common symptoms include difficulty following instructions, organizing time or tasks, listening to words directed to them, or making careless mistakes. Maintaining sustained mental focus for long periods can be harder than for neurotypical people. For the hyperactive-impulsive folks, you might struggle with impatience, waiting your turn, talking too much, or moving around excessively. You have so much energy, like a nonstop motor.

While one's behavior can characterize it, there's so much more going on that others don't see. Most ADHD symptoms lie beneath the surface, like emotional dysregulation, irritability, racing thoughts, flight of ideas, and more.

DIAGNOSIS

While there is no singular test for ADHD, most clinicians will look at more than just a questionnaire. Done right, it may take several sessions for the doctor to familiarize themselves with you, the patient, to ascertain if they have ADHD accurately. Overall, a child must meet a minimum of six out of nine total DSM-V symptoms, significantly if such symptoms have impacted their home and school life.

Unfortunately, there is a modern trend in which ADHD is largely over diagnosed yet misdiagnosed. Concerned adults might over-worry about their child who can't seem to sit still, sometimes taking them prematurely to get checked, leaving with a prescription. The issue is that people have different definitions of hyperactivity, and children are naturally high-energy and need different activities to keep them stimulated. On the other hand, other parents may not detect a problem in their children, especially if they seem to be doing well in school. Once they become a teen or adult, they may use substances like caffeine, alcohol, or other drugs to manage their undetected ADHD.

Older teens and adults are diagnosed differently because we learn better to mask some more obvious behavioral symptoms as we age. They need only 5 out of 9 symptoms to qualify for a diagnosis, and those symptoms must appear in more than one setting (they are not context-dependent).

At least 4.4% of adults in the United States have been diagnosed with ADHD. Diagnosing adults is very different from diagnosing children. For one, children tend to present more of the obvious external symptoms. On the other hand, adults have more toned-down outward symptoms, and most of their ADHD is unseen by others. For instance, they may struggle more with emotional disregulation, cognitive abilities, executive functioning, and sleep problems.

My diagnosis did not happen until later in my life. It confirmed that I had suspected that I had mostly AD (attention deficit) and a little HD (hyperactivity). My first big realization was my lack of focus and ability to accomplish daily tasks. Luckily, in the last 20 years, I have pursued a healthy diet and exercise fanatically. I attribute these healthy practices to my milder symptoms. I can chart my more difficult times with my ADHD and pinpoint the less healthy periods in my life.

All of these beneficial habits have helped me inspire the holistic suggestions in this book, alternately or alongside conventional ADHD treatments. Once I understood and faced my ADHD, I implemented more beneficial practices, going as far as becoming a vegan. After years of personal research, I understood that most diseases, even brain fog, result from inflammation. There is no better way to eliminate inflammation than eliminating animal products from your diet; bonus — a vegan diet is also good for the earth/climate. Exercise has always been a cornerstone in my life, but scheduling and having clear goals have been game changers in my fitness. As I slide into my late fifties, I am fitter than I was in my teens and twenties. I believe that making healthy choices can create a solid foundation for well-being and mental clarity.

TREATMENT

The first solution that comes to mind for ADHD is stimulants or prescription medications. Who hasn't heard of Adderall, after all? It's a widespread belief that ADHD is a brain-based disorder; it can't be fixed with anything other than a chemical, neurotransmitter-targeting drug. That could not be farther from the truth. Overall, treatments for ADHD fall into the following categories:
1. Medication
2. Behavior therapy/Counseling
3. Alternative treatments

MEDICATION

The first line of treatment for ADHD is medication. Two types are available: stimulant or non-stimulant medications. Stimulants are fast-acting and work similarly to caffeine, releasing dopamine and other energy-inducing neurotransmitters that help focus. Non-stimulants take at least a week to set in and may not work for everyone.

Medication is beneficial for children, but can also help adults get relief from their symptoms, enough to ride the momentum into improving other parts of their life through skill-building. After all, medication doesn't treat all aspects of ADHD that most people don't mention, like academic and study skills, improving interpersonal communication, and work performance.

BEHAVIOR-BASED THERAPY

While ADHD isn't a behavior disorder — meaning a learned set of maladaptive behavior that can be unlearned, you can improve and support your brain with therapy like cognitive-behavioral therapy. Cognitive-behavioral therapy merges thoughts, emotions, and behaviors to recondition yourself to learn supportive skills.

COUNSELING: NEVER BE AFRAID TO ASK FOR HELP

Sometimes life can be overwhelming and feels bigger than we can manage alone. In that case, seeking professional help through counseling is always wise. A licensed therapist can help navigate your mental health and determine the possible need for medication.

Tips for finding the right therapist for you:

1. Do an online search of a reliable database; American Psychological Association; www.GoodTherapy.com ; www.psychologytoday.com
2. Does the provider specialize in ADHD?
3. Do they take your insurance?
4. Read reviews, as these are the best indicator of the provider's style.
5. Check the provider's credentials.
6. Search locally; state and country mental wellness agencies are a great start.
7. Ask your general doctor or trusted friends for local recommendations.
8. Make an appointment and give them a try; if it's not a good fit, try another provider.

ALTERNATIVE TREATMENTS

The alternative treatments are basically a miscellaneous box of solutions that don't fall under clinically provided treatments. These include commercial herbal supplements like fish oil, nootropics that act as natural, non-prescription stimulants, brain-supporting diets, and lifestyle fixes like exercise and mindfulness.

No one treatment is better than the other. Always look to your doctor or professional's opinion first, as everyone's needs differ. More severe cases will require professional support throughout the treatment process. However, I believe that the best way to address ADHD is through a mixture of all three. If medication or therapy are not options, I recommend combining various alternative treatments to create a holistic lifestyle change to support yourself.

EMBRACING ADHD

ADHD symptoms are no secret to you. For too long, you've experienced the debilitating effects of difficulty focusing, fluctuating moods, and whims. You have quickly drained energy when trudging through the daily grind of a "normal" life, only a project away from burnout.

Maybe you felt neutral about ADHD or felt like it was a huge burden on your shoulders. You're frustrated by your self-sabotage. ADHD can feel like it holds you back in a lot of ways. That's what happened to me, especially when I did not understand what I was doing wrong or why my brain seemed to work so differently compared to others. If this is you right now, I'd like you to consider a new perspective: embracing your ADHD and claiming it as your own.

Often, we tend to over-identify with ADHD and all the labels it comes with. However, identification usually leads to taking all the negative aspects and making them defining parts of our lives and personalities. At the same time, you may reject those parts of yourself. For instance, you might struggle with sudden anger outbursts that make you feel guilty and ashamed afterward. Those feelings can create the urge to avoid or hide the problem. It brings you pain, so you reject it as a part of your identity. In doing so, however, you cannot fix the root of it. Everyone feels anger, and if you were to accept that, on some level, that anger is still real to you, but your ADHD may amplify it, then you can proceed more deliberately in reducing outbursts.

Accepting the ADHD part of yourself allows you to adjust your life to your goal of being yourself. If you can't switch it off, it's only best to use it to your advantage. Think of an athlete or an artist that has ADHD and has reframed it positively.

Moreover, you can also let go of the toxic need to conform or "be normal." In this world, "normal" doesn't exist. Average exists, but that means most people lean toward a certain state. To find the average, there also needs to be outliers. So many people in history have been "outliers" (in a positive, beneficial sense). I bet you have thought to yourself, "I don't want to be like others, either. I want to stand out and be different." Embrace that inner child. [2]

As we grow older, this desire gets deterred by social pressures. We forget the underdogs' struggles, the criticism, and the shunning. Even if it isn't outright, many people with ADHD experience some judgment, either from either or from inwards, about how different they are. Why can't I do this task like others' can so naturally? Why has this become so difficult for me? Why am I always struggling when everyone else has moved on or has their head on straight? These may have been frequent thoughts you've had. By the time you're an adult, you want to be normal (**Neurotypical** is the right word.)

People don't make this easier, which we're better off coming to terms with. If you are an inattentive type who often resides in your imagination, others may see someone spaced out, bored, or disinterested. They don't see the flood of new, lush ideas swimming around your head, waiting for you to go home and hyperfocus on a beautiful painting, sculpture, writing, or whatever your creative preference is. When they see that you jump to impulsive actions like dominating the conversation or taking a spontaneous trip to the city next door, they may think you are flighty, directionless, or lack self-control. They don't see your assertive nature in business; always jumping into massive action before further doubt can make you procrastinate. Accepting your ADHD means knowing who you are regardless of what people think. That will make you stronger.

Other than the fact that none of history's greatest artists, athletes, thinkers, and famous people were "normal," they know that you don't have to be neurotypical to achieve and do things as well as they can. The world may not be built for you. However, you can support yourself to better adapt to the world. When you embrace yourself completely, ADHD and all, you can tap into your inner drive and learn to address your most pressing concerns.

FROM WEAKNESS TO SUPERPOWER

How do you turn your ADHD drive "flaws" into your own superpowers? First, you must take all the labels you've tacked on and turn them on their heads. How can you make something that has plagued you, like scattered focus or restlessness, into something useful?

THE DANGERS OF LABELING

Labels help recognize and categorize issues that could use extra support. At the same time, we must remember that labels are not perfect. Not everyone fits perfectly in the ADHD box. Sometimes "gifted" students may look like they have ADHD because of the overlapping signs. Mislabeling or over-identifying with a label can affect adolescents and adults throughout their lives.

Some may focus too much on how limiting their ADHD-drive "weaknesses" are, thinking of only how much it sets them apart. Perhaps they see themselves as abnormal, disordered, weird, or broken. It is in this way that ADHD can derail a person's self-esteem.

Understanding the nuance is the key to breaking away from the negative connotations of ADHD. Every trait has a good and bad extreme to it. Any weakness has another side that, if used correctly, can be an amazing strength or skill.

REFRAMING: HOW TO TURN NEGATIVE INTO POSITIVE

Avoiding the negative connotations of certain labels is not delusional. It's a mindset shift. Right now, your mind only sees a narrow aspect of yourself and your potential. If you were to challenge the labels that have been a part of your identity for so long, you might find surprising opportunities hidden. Research shows that when we expand our attention to see the whole picture, good or bad, we can better adopt a growth mindset rather than a fixed mindset. We can see ADHD as something that can work with us rather than against us.

- You are not hyperactive; you have an immense amount of vivacious energy.
- Rather than scattered, you are filled to the brim with creativity.
- Don't call your divided attention across multiple interests distracted; call it having a broad/creative perspective.
- Has anyone ever called you an adrenaline junky? They don't see or understand that you have the heart of an explorer; you take risks that most people are too hesitant to take.
- If anyone has ever called you crazy during your impassioned moments, the truth is you are inspired and full of a well of emotion.
- You are not obsessive or even OCD — you are passionate when hyper-focusing on something that gives you joy and purpose.

- Finally, the emotional disregulation that comes with ADHD does not make you sensitive or weak — it means that you can be more in tune with your inner being and more empathetic and compassionate with others because you feel so much.

Yes, many of these traits can have their downsides. However, if we focus more on the positive, bright sides, think of the potential they can give us. Getting rid of them completely would reduce the parts that make you who you are. What is important to remember is that just because ADHD is a condition that affects many people, it is presented in unique, individual ways.

What you call ADHD is actually just ADHD enhancing and highlighting already existing qualities in you. In a way, it's like the volume has been turned up for some of your best qualities. All you need to do is; gain control of the remote to turn the volume up or down, depending on the context. Going to an eleven may be perfectly appropriate if you are in a ski race. Never downplay your positive traits in an attempt to be normal. Normal is overrated!

While embracing ADHD is the first step, there's still a long, winding path to travel down. Your destination: Becoming more self-actualized in learning to manage your ADHD and your life. Because this is all about accepting ADHD as an inextricable part of who you are, one that you can live and thrive with, especially if you can balance your mind, body, and spirit. These three facets of life all affect and work with each other. When you gradually renovate each area, you are on your way to breaking past the limitations of ADHD and tapping into the potential.

In the next chapter, we will start with the first pillar of health: Our body.

Part One

THE BODY

Chapter 1

A Healthy Diet To Thrive

"Let food be thy medicine and medicine be thy food."

—Hippocrates, ancient Greek father of medicine

∾

W hat you eat is probably the most crucial decision you make each day. Your food choices will make the difference between having optimal energy with a sharp mind or low energy, brain fog, and over time, a diseased body. Our bodies are unique and complex systems that require healthy nutrients, clean water, and oxygen to thrive.

Back to basics, food is fuel, meant to be energy, like gasoline for a car. You can choose if you will run like a high-performance Ferrari or a rusted-out minivan with a failing transmission. It has been said, "Food is fuel, not entertainment." Food has many

psychological triggers and is often misused as a form of entertainment, comfort, and reward.

You can control how you fuel your body by educating yourself
on proper nutrition. Many people do not take this seriously
enough and eat like children on vacation. You owe it to yourself
to be responsible enough to feed yourself healthy food, creating
a body and mind that will perform at optimal levels and bring
vitality to your life. This single change will revolutionize your
overall well-being for the better. One of the best gifts you can
give your children is to be a great role model and teach them to
cook and eat healthy food. My daughter thanks me for giving her
these skills which has helped her maintain a healthy adult body.

The "mind-body connection" isn't just a buzzword: It's a real
phenomenon that describes the relationship between the body's
and brain's health. Eating food can help or exacerbate your
focus, attention, concentration, and executive functioning. Just as
nutrition is essential in treating other physical conditions, it plays
a strong role in managing ADHD.

As a teen and young adult, I was the poster child for trying every
fad diet out there. Low self-esteem and body dysmorphia led me
to unhealthy diets that exacerbated my ADHD symptoms. As I
reflect on my life timeline, I realize some of my most severe
symptoms were in my teens and twenties when I ate junk food,
sugary foods, yo-yo dieted, and drank too much coffee and
alcohol.

. . .

In this chapter, we will focus on how you can support yourself with and despite ADHD symptoms, by caring for your body, specifically through a diet that supports your well-being and does not add to your ADHD symptoms. Here, you will find information about a diet fit for ADHD needs, including practical tips on how to make lifestyle changes easier.

NUTRITION FACTS:
THE GOOD & THE BAD

THE GOOD: PROTEIN

Studies have proven that people without ADHD can improve their brain function with a nutritious diet. Imagine now a person with ADHD whose brain already functions differently from others. ADHD brains struggle more with memory, attention, concentration, and hyperactivity than usual. Therefore, it makes sense that controlling the diet is even more critical to provide the brain with better fuel.

Often, we can exacerbate our ADHD with our lifestyle or ways of coping. For instance, you might think sugary snacks (bars) help you with a rush of energy in moments of under stimulation, when you need to focus on a task. In the long run, those blood sugar spikes can be even more detrimental to your ability to control your attention.

Nutrition should be the foundation of your lifestyle changes. It affects so much of our health, both body and brain. Certain foods

5

can make ADHD symptoms worse or support the brain despite ADHD. You can take back the reins of your behavior when you eat a complete, balanced diet of complex carbs, vegetables, protein, and fruit and reduce detrimental foods.3

First, let's discuss the essential and healthy foods that will nourish your body and mind to help you manage your ADHD.

Eating enough protein is essential to managing our irregular bouts of energy. Not only that, but protein is the little-known building block for neurotransmitters. All the pieces involved in ADHD, like dopamine, norepinephrine, serotonin, and cortisol — all those parts of your brain chemistry — are made up of proteins. Eating sufficient protein results in better intercell communication. This helps fight brain fog, improves messages from your nerves to the brain, and allows you to think more efficiently. Protein also counteracts the negative effects of high blood sugar, which can increase hyperactivity and impulsivity. Focus on foods like grass-fed lean beef, fish, chicken, beans, eggs, nuts, and seeds. Again, I prefer vegan options for many reasons, but the choice of animal food sources is personal.

VITAMINS AND MINERALS

As soon as you are diagnosed with ADHD, I recommend getting tested for nutritional deficiencies. Most people can further suffer from attention and alertness issues due to lacking an essential vitamin or mineral. Figuring out what you are deficient in can help you tackle those problems faster with supplements. A few basic blood rests can give you a good baseline, and you can chart your healthy progress over the years.

Zinc, iron, and magnesium are just some nutrients that people with ADHD tend to be low in. Zinc regulates the neurotransmitter dopamine, which has a huge role in ADHD and reducing depression symptoms. Low vitamin D and iron are also correlated with ADHD, leading to sleeplessness, hyperactivity, difficulty focusing, and increased ADHD severity by at least 30%. Magnesium can settle one's agitation and hyperactivity, especially alongside medication.

Fill up on these vitamins through whole food sources with the following foods:

- Zinc: Meat, beans, nuts, shellfish
- Vitamin D: Fish, liver, egg yolks, mushrooms, and fortified plant-based milk
- Iron: Beef, liver, kidney beans, and tofu Magnesium: Almonds, spinach, peanuts, pumpkin seeds
- Or try a good supplement (after consulting your doctor).

OMEGA-3

As an essential fat source, omega-3 fatty acids are necessary for proper brain function. Most children with ADHD don't have enough omega-3 fats. First of all, the brain is 60% fat. Additionally, if you don't have enough omega-3 fatty acids, your neurons degenerate and don't generate enough serotonin to manage mood. Moreover, your dopamine needs properly formed cellular receptors (which are the landing areas for nerve signals) to receive communication from other neurons to boost Omega- 3s, the American Psychological Association recommends consuming fish twice a week, but for those with ADHD, you will need to supplement your diet with flax-seed capsules or fish oil. [2]

THE BAD
SUGAR

For ADHD kids, high sugar intake can increase hyperactivity and agitation to an extreme degree. ADHD folks may be at higher risk for sugar addiction, and it can mess with your energy and mood levels. Using sugar as a pick-me-up, be it through chocolate bars, soda, juice, elaborate coffee drinks, or granola bars, know that your energy boost will only be temporary and you will become dependent. Over time, you may struggle with worse inattention.[3]

Sugar may also contribute to a cesspool of bad bacteria in your gut that leads to all sorts of inflammation, especially when combined with chronic stress.

If you take nothing from these nutrition tips, take at least this: reduce your sugar intake! Avoid or reduce foods that include the following: high-fructose corn syrup, cane juice, dextrin, dextrose, maltodextrin, sucrose, molasses, and malt syrup.

. . .

In the early nighties, I learned about the negative effects of sugar and quickly adopted a low sugar diet. Eating no sugar is almost impossible, as many prepared foods have sugar as the main ingredient. Learn to read food labels and choose whole food that is not in boxes, cans, or jars whenever possible.

THE ROLE OF INFLAMMATION

Inflammation is a state in which your body heals itself against foreign invaders or illness using fighter inflammatory antibodies. It's a healthy response, but, like anything else, too much means bad news. In the case of chronic inflammation, the immune response is repeatedly triggered more often than it should, and most times for no reason at all. Your internal body's danger meter is broken, the alarm blaring every hour. Inflammatory cells are always flooding your body and finding nothing of substance to attack, begin attacking your internal organs.

Chronic inflammation is present in many disorders like arthritis and cancer. Almost every disease has inflammatory origins. Even chronic stress can lead to inflammation that can impact your health, leading to poor skin health, digestive issues, hair loss, headaches, fatigue, reduced energy levels, sleep disorders, and mysterious pain.

THE MECHANICS BEHIND INFLAMMATION

Did you know that your brain can be inflamed? The symptoms include brain fog, slow thinking, and even irritability, anger,

9

depression, memory loss, and overall fatigue. Ever had a song stuck in your head? That may point to possible inflammation.[4] Pro-inflammatory cytokines are produced and interfere with the brain environment, causing cognitive and behavioral symptoms.[5]

While brain inflammation can be triggered by an acute injury, it can also be caused by overall chronic inflammation in the body due to poor diet, food intolerances, chronic stress, diabetes or regular high blood sugar, and a leaky gut. See how the mind and body are so connected?

THE DANGER OF INFLAMMATION

Inflammation essentially reduces the speed and efficiency of neurons communicating with each other. This slows down connections and messages, creating that feeling of "brain fog." The same thing occurs in depression (which adults with ADHD are at risk for), in which cytokines (immune cells triggered during inflammation) reduce serotonin, thus affecting brain function and mood.

When affected, brain cells can be destroyed: there is literally less of your brain. Moreover, chronic stress (which, as you'll soon find out, goes hand-in-hand with inflammation) has been shown to deteriorate gray matter as you age gradually — yes, your brain volume actually decreases. In the long term, it can lead to faster brain aging and a risk of degenerative disorders like Parkinson's, Alzheimer's, and dementia. In other words, brain inflammation speeds up cognitive decline.[5]

. . .

There is so much new research on anti-Inflammatory lifestyles and has been the focus of my lay research lately. It is worth researching by listening to some podcasts or watching a few YouTube videos to dip your toe into the subject to learn how you can set yourself up for better health as you age.

HOW INFLAMMATION RELATES TO ADHD AND WORSENS SYMPTOMS

Science tells us that inflammation in the brain contributes to neurological disorders, ADHD being one of them.

Like most things, inflammation (brain or otherwise) may have a cyclical relationship with ADHD. There is an inextricable presence of anxiety among those with ADHD. Many people with these conditions find stress and anxiety to be a factor in their lives. In fact, people with ADHD are 50% more likely also to have an anxiety disorder. ADHD can ramp up your stress in everyday situations that can seem so simple to neurotypical people. Furthermore, anxiety and chronic stress can build up into chronic brain and body inflammation because stressors always trigger the immune response.

Adults with ADHD are more prone to frustration, usually at themselves. This can be caused by perfectionism or by the fact that they developed a mistrust towards themselves about their reliability. For instance, you may feel even more stress about an upcoming deadline because you don't know if you will be able to get into a hyper-focused flow state, or you'll procrastinate until the very last few hours beforehand.

. . .

There is an emotional disregulation side of ADHD, wherein it is much harder to manage and fall out from high emotions. High emotional states can affect our brains in the long term. In both the short-term and the long-term, you feel brain fog, a common component of ADHD that is characterized by slow thinking. It feels almost like your thoughts are walking through thick, heavy mud, slowing you down. This is not a simple case of temporary fatigue; it results from inflammation caused by habits like your diet.

ALCOHOL, CAFFEINE & DRUG SENSITIVITIES

Other than diet, it's important to address other substances you consume and how they affect your ADHD. Because of the nature of ADHD, you may be more sensitive to certain substances, specifically alcohol and caffeine. Whether you supplement your diet with them to cope or your ADHD impulses push you towards risky behavior when it comes to recreational drugs, reducing them or cutting them out entirely will be necessary for the overall improvement of your symptoms.

ALCOHOL & ADHD RISK FACTORS

If you have ADHD, you may have struggled with (or be at risk for) using various methods to cope with your symptoms, whether you are aware or not. One popular method is, of course, substance use. Alcohol use and abuse, in particular, are no strangers to ADHD adults. While not everyone falls into this camp, people with ADHD are at higher risk of not only starting to drink earlier but also be more likely to misuse it, binge drink, and even be more affected by alcohol's effects. In fact, research has shown a strong correlation between severe ADHD in childhood and earlier drinking behavior.[5]

Alcohol dependence can create a harsh cycle in which drinking serves as a way to dampen ADHD symptoms, but later it can make those symptoms more uncontrollable, like impulsiveness, risk-taking, and difficulty focusing. The danger of alcohol abuse lies in the long-term: Alcoholism causes rampant cognitive problems and memory issues and hinders decision-making.

ADHD & ADDICTION

The unfortunate truth is that adults with ADHD are far more likely to become addicted to certain substances, be they alcohol or drugs. Impulsivity can lead to risky, you-only-live-once behavior, leading to bad judgment regarding substance use. Sometimes ADHD, especially when undiagnosed for a long time, can flow over into other parts of your life, affecting your job, education, relationships, and overall emotional stability. This can lead to using, abusing, and depending on substances as a coping mechanism. If you have ADHD and are dealing with substance abuse or addiction, you must address that; get sober first before managing your ADHD. [6]

Chapter 1

EFFECT OF CAFFEINE ON BRAIN & BODY

One of the biggest questions I have seen people with ADHD ask — as I, too, have asked — how does caffeine affect a brain with ADHD? Considering that it is a stimulant, in the same pharmaceutical category as top ADHD medications, could it actually help manage symptoms on a low-grade level?

Caffeine does have beneficial effects on the brain and body by helping anyone keep fatigue at bay and hone their focus on the moment. It also clears up minor headaches, improves mental sharpness and memory, and can even protect against certain diseases in the long-term. These advantages are relevant to just about anyone.

However, just like any other substance, natural or otherwise, caffeine has its dangers. Taking more than a moderate amount of caffeine daily (depending on the individual) can lead to increased anxiety, heart palpitations, restlessness, headaches, and even muscle tremors. You may feel sick to your stomach and agitated. Caffeine taken throughout the day, over a long period, can completely skew your sleep schedule, and nights will be much longer for you.

Now, what if you have ADHD? If caffeine makes neurotypical people more energized and alert, does it do the opposite for those with ADHD? Since it's a stimulant, would it not work the same as ADHD medication? The answer to these questions is: It depends.

. . .

For many people with ADHD, caffeine can offer a slight reprieve from distracted focus and inattention. It may be true that many adults with ADHD have knowingly or unknowingly turned to regular coffee use to abate their symptoms. However, it affects each person differently. Some may experience even greater rest-lessness and hyperactivity, pushing them to take risks they other-wise wouldn't (to a small extent), like speaking more than usual during a work meeting without regard for what their supervisors or coworkers might think. For others, caffeine can exacerbate their mental chatter and overall sense of anxiety. [7]

What is concerning is that because caffeine has a temporary effect, adults with ADHD who have been masking for a long time trying to fit in with their fellow high-functioning neurotypi-cals can become dependent. They might start with a cup a day, which can become four cups, and a few afternoon Red Bulls to get through life years later.

As the body becomes used to caffeine's effects, you will need more to feel the same relief. This can spill into your long-term sleep patterns, making you chronically tired and stressed. Not to mention, when combined with chronic stress and lack of proper rest, long-term caffeine dependence can throw your adrenals into a tailspin, with more cortisol than necessary being pumped out daily.

HOW DOES CAFFEINE AFFECT ADHD?

While caffeine can help with balancing dopamine levels in ADHD brains, it isn't recommended to manage ADHD. [8] Just because it is a stimulant does not mean it, would be effective as a treatment on its own. Why would there be any need for Adderall, then? Actually, to even come close to reducing ADHD symptoms using caffeine, the amount needed would cause extreme agitation and restlessness.

You must mind your caffeine levels if you have ADHD and are already taking medication. On the positive side, stimulant medications can effectively kill any craving or desire you might have for caffeine. On the other hand, taking other forms of caffeine while taking medication can cause jittery nerves.

Remember that a holistic outlook is a key to ADHD management. Don't just rely on stimulants, prescribed or otherwise. Use a combination of caffeine, omega-3 fatty acids, and zinc and vitamin D supplements to fortify your brain.

WHOLE-FOODS PLANT-BASED (WFPB) DIET

Based on everything we know about diets supporting ADHD, a whole-foods plant-based diet is most recommended for a complete lifestyle turnaround. By focusing on whole foods — natural, grown, whole ingredients (rather than processed), you can maximize the variety and quantity of nutrients to take in.

WHAT IS A WFPB DIET EXACTLY?

To follow a WFPB diet, all you have to do is toss out anything processed or refined. Get the majority of the food you eat as close to its original, most natural forms as possible. For example, instead of a processed natural, vegan energy bar made of dates or dried fruit, nuts, and seed, eat a mixture of those ingredients in their original forms for long-lasting energy. While not vegan, a WFPB does limit animal products, although it's flexible. It's a personal decision to eat whatever meat you desire, as long as it is free-range poultry and eggs or organic, grass-fed beef, or freshly caught fish. Quality is key. [9]

WFPB EFFECTS

A whole foods plant-based diet can improve your overall health, help you lose weight if needed, and bring down your inflammation markers (C-Reactive protein test). For ADHD specifically, a whole foods diet can fight against cognitive decline, a major risk. Due to the antioxidants in various plants, you can fight against the free radicals associated with inflammation. Most importantly, you can balance your blood sugar levels to have more stable moods and behavior.

You can enjoy many benefits by nourishing your brain and body with whole foods. I have been vegan for over 5 years now and have really noticed a vast improvement of my overall health and lack of inflammation in my joints. This is a huge plus as I age, with previous joint issues from my active life.

. . .

Chapter 1

WHAT TO EAT

To follow the WFPB diet, here's a (non-exhaustive) list of foods you can eat:

- **Carbohydrates**: Fruits, vegetables, starchy vegetables, whole grains
- **Protein**: Plant-based protein, eggs, free-range chicken, tofu, tempeh, moderate amounts of beef, sheep, game, etc.
- **Fats:** Fatty fish, legumes, seeds, nuts, nut butter, healthy fats, legumes
- **Other:** Unsweetened coconut milk, almond milk, cashew milk, spices/herbs: basil, rosemary, turmeric, curry, black pepper, salt
- **Condiments**: Salsa, mustard, nutritional yeast, soy sauce, vinegar, lemon juice
- **Drinks**: Coffee, tea, sparkling water

Avoid

- Fast food
- Fried food and partially hydrogenated oils
- Added sugars and sweets
- Refined grains
- Packaged and convenience foods
- Processed vegan-friendly foods
- Artificial sweeteners
- Processed animal products

HOW TO CREATE A SOLID MEAL PLAN

As someone with ADHD, I know how hard it can be to carry out a major lifestyle change. Carrying out a change amid the endless stream of ideas in your head can be challenging. Remembering to eat the right foods can be hard when you're feeling bored, tired, or impulsive. However, easy organization tips can set you up for success.

First, create a menu for every day of the week. Some folks with ADHD may do better with a similar weekly meal plan full of their favorite foods. List out what you will eat for the week; google some healthy recipes and create a shopping list. To help you better follow your meal plan, prepare your ingredients beforehand. Do some meal prep at the end of each week by batch-cooking, washing, chopping vegetables, and placing them in air-tight containers lined with paper towels. This is my weekly hack for making quick salads throughout the week; vegetables will stay fresh that way.

STRUCTURING YOUR DIET TO SUIT YOUR LIFESTYLE

If you think a whole foods plant-based diet might limit or stop you from enjoying your favorite foods, think again. Just about any of your favorite dishes can be modified to meet the WFPB diet guidelines. Here's an example day in recipes you can try to give you a jumpstart.

. . .

Chapter 1

BREAKFAST: Bean, Potato & Veggie Vegan Breakfast Hash [10]

This savory breakfast is just filling enough to keep you revving until your next meal, with a healthy combination of protein and carbs to keep your blood sugar levels steady. With this rich breakfast hash, you won't miss your eggs and bacon (if that's your thing). You can use an air fryer to cut down on oil.

INGREDIENTS:
- 3 large russet potatoes cubed
- 2 teaspoons oil
- 1/2 teaspoon salt
- 1/4 teaspoon black pepper
- 1 can beans
- 2 cups baby spinach
- 1 medium chopped zucchini
- 1 medium chopped squash
- 1 chopped red bell pepper
- 1/2 cup sliced mushrooms
- 1 1/2 teaspoon garlic powder
- 1 1/2 teaspoon onion powder
- 1/2 teaspoon smoked paprika
- 1 pinch of chili flakes

DIRECTIONS:

1. Heat oil in a skillet on medium heat and throw in cubed potatoes with some salt and pepper.
2. Stir the potatoes for about half an hour or until browned.
3. Toss in all the other ingredients and spices, excluding the spinach and beans since they cook the fastest. Cook for about 10 minutes.
4. Finally, add spinach leaves and beans and stir for about 4 more minutes.
5. Feel free to top it off with ketchup, salsa, or avocado. You can also use corn tortillas to make a mini breakfast taco!

LUNCH: Curried Chickpea Salad [11]

If you're not a salad fan, I'm certain this recipe will convince you. With a mixture of sweet and savory, plus the robust flavor of chickpeas and creamy cashews, this recipe is excellent for a slow weekend lunch, or an on-the-go meal. [11]

INGREDIENTS:
Salad:
2 cups of chickpeas
(alternately, this can be made with mashed tofu)
1/2 cup of raisins
1 cup of diced celery
1/2 cup of chopped apples
1/2 cup of chopped scallions

Chapter 1

Chopped greens

Sauce:
1/2 cup of soaked cashews
8 raisins, soaked
1/2 fresh squeezed lemon juice
1 tablespoon of curry powder
A pinch of sea salt
½ teaspoon of honey

DIRECTIONS:

1. To create the sauce, throw all the ingredients into a blender with a few spoonfuls of water; the finished result should be smooth
2. Grind the chickpeas in a bowl with a masher or fork until thick and chunky
3. Combine the chickpeas with the sauce
4. Add in the rest of the salad ingredients
5. Mix this salad onto a bed of greens or eat it alone in a pita pocket.

DINNER: Creamy Plant-Based Avocado Pasta [12]

Trust me, you won't have to fear craving pasta or carbs while eating to support your ADHD. Create a balanced pasta dish by focusing on a sauce of healthy fats in the form of avocado.

. . .

INGREDIENTS:
- 1 1/4 cup of water
- 2 ripe avocados
- 1 cup of basil
- 1 dozen cherry tomatoes
- 1 lb. of brown rice pasta of choice
- 1 garlic clove
- 1 lemon
- 1 teaspoon of maple syrup
- A pinch of salt
- A pinch of black pepper

DIRECTIONS:

1. Get your pasta to a boil according to the package directions
2. Throw in avocados, 1 cup of basil, garlic, lemon, maple syrup, salt, black pepper, and water into a blender or food processor to make your creamy sauce
3. Pour the sauce over the cooked pasta, mixing if desired
4. Top it all off with cherry tomatoes (cut into halves) and the remaining 1/2 of basil
5. Eat like you're dining in a fancy Italian restaurant!

These meals are mouthwatering enough for even your non-whole-food-diet-consuming friends and family to enjoy.

There's no doubt that your eating habits can affect both your mood and behavior. Switching to a healthy regime for ADHD is a no-brainer since diet is such a powerful influence on your health. We have all gotten the memo on this and know it to be true. Don't wait for major medical or psychological problems to face facts. Make a positive change to your diet now, and within a month, you will be reaping the rewards. Of course, you can't forget other ways to keep your body in good shape and maintain mind-body balance. In the next chapter, we'll build your arsenal with strategies to boost your physical health.

∾

"You are what you eat—so don't be fast, cheap, easy, or fake." —Unknown

Chapter 2

Consistent Exercise For Mental Clarity

"A Body in Motion Will Remain in Motion."
-- Sir Issac Newton

❧

According to Sir Isaac Newton's first law of motion, "A Body in Motion Will Remain in Motion." This wonderful reminder that staying active, will become a way of life, benefitting our bodies for years to come.

Humans evolved from running to hunt and gathering by working on farms. Unfortunately, the creature comforts of modern life can cause us harm. Constant driving and not walking deprive our bodies of exercise that could burn off calories. Television is also a primary culprit that has made us more sedentary. Binge-watching TV series, night after night, and not working our muscles, creates weaker bodies and fuzzy thinking.

. . .

Both cardio and weight-bearing exercise is necessary for a young body but essential as you age, especially if you want to walk in your eighties. Exercise and sports work as therapy for your mind and are the key to assisting in the production of serotonin and dopamine to regulate our moods and mental well-being. Additionally, the excess energy we have from our hyperactivity can help to fuel our sporty and active lifestyle, and there is no superpower more wonderful than that!

Eating healthy is a huge piece of your ADHD-supporting lifestyle change. It's just the beginning, though. Keeping your body in excellent fitness is another part of the equation. More research has shown its immense effect on thinking and emotional health as well — both for neurotypical and ADHD communities. I attribute a lot of my success in life to the effects of exercise on my mental health and clarity.

THE EFFECTS OF REGULAR EXERCISE

Generally, exercise provides a wealth of advantages for *everyone*. Just a few benefits include:

Maintain a healthy weight: Your body is your home for life. A healthy weight is important for you to experience positive well-being and avoid the risks of various disorders. Regular exercise and increasing movement contribute to keeping your body weight in line. Try more overall activity by taking the stairs(cliche, but it works), having a nice morning dance before breakfast, or taking a long hike instead of a car ride.

· · ·

Improved mood: Moving your body can trigger a cascade of positive neurotransmitters that make you feel better instantly and throughout your day. Exercise has an antidepressant effect on your brain due to the adrenaline rush. You feel powerful, sinuous, and unstoppable. Regular exercise, of course, can do wonders for your self-esteem, either due to you feeling good about being in shape or looking good. A positive self-concept is important for us to accept ourselves, a powerful tool for our daily confidence.

Boosts energy: If you are out of shape, it can dampen your spirits and limit the activities you can do. Consistent movement and exercise increase your baseline energy levels because your body gets stronger to adapt to the energy you are putting out.

Improves sleep quality: Sleep helps your brain work as effectively as possible. Daily exercise helps you maintain a steady sleep schedule that balances your mood and gives you the mental energy you need to stay alert and concentrated throughout the day.[1]

EXERCISE BENEFITS FOR ADHD

The main reason why exercise can help us with ADHD is that it can balance critical hormones. Brains with ADHD are known for generating less dopamine than they should. Dopamine is the critical part of the machinery that can help you stay focused on a task to meet a desired goal or reward. Without it, thinking clearly can be completely shot.

. . .

Exercising is one natural way to increase your default dopamine stores. Simultaneously, it balances norepinephrine, a key neurotransmitter involved in alertness and energy, thus reducing your likelihood of becoming snappish, quickly reactive, or quick to frustration. Additionally, exercise offsets the overactive cerebellum's effects, reducing the restless need always to keep moving and fidgeting.[2]

This miraculous benefits of exercise over brain chemicals translates to many benefits, like the following examples:

EASES STRESS, AND ANXIETY

Anxiety is no stranger to adults with ADHD trying to function in the real world and being torn by hundreds of different responsibilities. Many of us can fall victim to chronic stress and day-to-day overwhelm; our senses can swing between under-stimulation and overstimulation, and we often meet our limit for the stress that we can take. Young people in their twenties, like my daughter, are more prone to anxiety with the myriad of new responsibilities and demands from our modern world. 'Adulting' can be plain overwhelming for many millennials. The T-shirt that reads 'Adulting- Would Not Recommend" with a one star rating, is both humorous and real. Many folks may just need more serotonin and dopamine.

With a regular exercise schedule, we can have overall higher secretions of positive neurotransmitters like serotonin and dopamine, which makes us feel better, calmer, and more centered. During exercise itself, it can feel like a brain massage.

Your brain gets a well-needed break, similar to the effect that stimulant medication can provide. Physical activity in the morning allows me to release energy and to be more focused once I sit down to my computer work.

An additional benefit of exercise, especially of the high-intensity type, is that you can more easily fall into the flow state: a period of intense concentration and creativity marked by alpha waves in your brain. The flow state is essentially effortless attention to work and gives us a gift of calm and productivity. I used to teach 6:00 AM spinning classes, and afterward, I felt euphoric, walking on clouds for the rest of the day. YAAAY dopamine!

IMPROVE IMPULSE CONTROL

Exercise has been known to combat the impulsivity, anxiety, depression, and hyperactivity of people with ADHD studies have shown.[3]

One such research tested participants' level of ability to delay discounting, which is when you can choose between a smaller reward now or a bigger reward later. Those who tend to choose the sooner rewards are high in impulsivity, which, as we all know, is a major ADHD struggle. This ties back to how the present moment is more valuable to us because it feels more real than the vague future. However, this impulsivity gets us into trouble and correlates with health and mental health concerns like obesity and addiction.[4]

Chapter 2

BOOST EXECUTIVE FUNCTION

Working out, specifically aerobic exercise or cardio, is one natural way to improve your executive function overall. Aerobic activities that require little thought and resistance training have fewer cognitive benefits. Performing an exercise that requires greater mental participation builds the strength of your executive functioning skills. Why? Because such physical activity requires the use of self-control, managing your response to the high intensity, and going on even when it gets hard. Yet it's stimulating enough to keep you engaged. Think of exercise like HIIT, which is relatively short but requires small bursts of your greatest power, strength, and speed.

BDNF & HIIT EXERCISE

Brain-derived neurotrophic factor (BDNF) is an aspect of the brain that maintains brain cells' overall health and communication. In essence, it helps with brain development and neuroplasticity.[5] If you don't have enough BDNF, it can result in anxiety, depression, and other mental health issues. Amazingly, aerobic exercise, specifically moderate-to-high intensity exercise, can boost BDNF. High-intensity interval training (HIIT) has more benefits.

While the circulation of BDNF right after exercise can be temporary, regular exercise over a few months increases not only BDNF but also the management of glucose levels.[6]

· · ·

THE RIGHT EXERCISE TO DO AND WHAT TO AVOID

I have found, and research supports, that exercise requiring the presence of the mind can be most beneficial. Even though we can assume any exercise helps improve overall concentration, for people with ADHD, a relatively low-effort exercise, with little thinking necessary, doesn't make as much of a difference as other types. Consider exercising on a treadmill; while it's healthy for the physical body, it quickly becomes just another tedious task. In contrast, running with interval training can keep your brain engaged much more than just steady running or jogging.

Virtually all types of exercise can support ADHD–here are some of my favorites:

AEROBIC EXERCISE

Running, biking, walking, and swimming are all excellent choices for aerobic exercise. In children alone, just 20 minutes of aerobic exercise can help them better inhibit maladaptive behavior and improve educational performance. I always thought that school should start with recess! Other forms of aerobic exercises include cycling, rowing, dancing, kickboxing, and any cardio machine at the gym. However, I would recommend exercising in various locations rather than just at your gym, which can quickly become boring. Try alternating your schedule with jogs in nature, a trip to the beach or woods, or try a variety of dance and fitness classes to keep things fresh and interesting.

. . .

The latest research indicates that you don't need to spend a lot of time doing aerobic exercise. Rather, the intensity of exertion is the most important component. Try a 15-minute intensive HIIT-High-Intensity Interval Training session. You can find many HIIT workouts for cycling or aerobic-type workouts on YouTube. The most important thing is to get out-of-breath and push yourself for short bursts (30-60 seconds), alternating with short recovery periods.

MARTIAL ARTS

Karate, taekwondo, jiu-jitsu, or judo: The martial arts engage your strength, brain, and technical skills. Whether you practice moves on your own or use them against an opponent, you train your brain and body to stay focused and synchronize. According to research, incredibly complex forms of physical activity can increase norepinephrine naturally. That includes martial arts, which includes technical movements that can simultaneously turn on multiple parts of the brain. For instance; understanding and correcting errors; comprehending risks and making decisions; having greater control of motor skills, and managing focused bouts of concentration at a time all experience improvements. The martial arts are an especially wonderful exercise practice for the ADHD brain!

STRENGTH TRAINING

Lunges, squats, pushups, and weights—any resistance training that works your muscles has a wealth of benefits for more than just your physique. Lifting weights can strengthen the brain's memory and learning center, the hippocampus. If you have any brain inflammation, regular strength training can rebuild the brain through neuroplasticity, its amazing power to change and adapt, for better or worse, to external stimuli.8 It reorganizes itself to re-grow the parts of the brain affected by inflammation, bad habits, and brain fog, along with any natural cognitive decline in later life.[9] It also doesn't hurt that strength training can improve your muscle tone, leading to improved self-concept and higher self-esteem. That's something we could all use, ADHD or not!

TEAM SPORTS

Is there any exercise you should avoid? Not necessarily, but sports, in general, quickly turn boring and fail to hold a person's attention for a long time. To combat this myself, I cycle through various activities, some days opting for hiking in the mountains, others taking a dance or Pilates class. Alternate your activities by time, sometimes going at it in the morning, and others in the evening, whatever works best for your day. Above all, maintain consistency and persistence over time for success! A good idea is to do a new sport every season to keep things exciting, like cross-country skiing in the winter and mountain biking in the summer.

A note of caution for those who like adrenaline or extreme sports. Activities like mountaineering, climbing, extreme down-hill mountain biking, and bungee jumping can appeal to the impulsive part of your brain. With adrenaline sports, you might get caught up in the thrill, take unwarranted risks with little hesitation, and end up in the ER, unable to exercise for months.

. . .

HOW TO CREATE A SUCESSFUL EXERCISE ROUTINE

As with anything else, it's important to structure your exercise of choice with your life. Reduce as many obstacles as possible, and remember that putting in your session will only make you more stable and efficient with ADHD. To do so, set up a weekly quota recommendation, implement exercise into your daily schedule, and focus more on intensity rather than duration to maximize its benefits for ADHD. You can set exercise dates with friends to inspire you and keep you accountable as well. Remember, consistency wins overall.

WEEKLY RECOMMENDED QUOTA

The first tip I recommend is to give yourself a weekly exercise quota. According to research-based advice, the optimal amount of exercise you need per week to achieve great benefits to health and ADHD symptoms is at least 150 minutes. That's about half an hour of moderate exercise daily, five days a week. My quota is almost double that since exercise is a part of my job and life-style. Also, I have come to love the good feelings and benefits of endorphins and dopamine I get from exercise.

DAILY STRUCTURE

Strive to work out nearly every day, except for rest days, although I like to do some light yoga or walking on those days too. Exercising in the morning is a common recommendation since it can give you an energizing start to your day and provide something to look forward to. Many of us with ADHD struggle severely with waking up early. It can be the bane of our existence. Adding exercise to our morning routine may be just the thing to get us instantly alert and ready for the day to come. Exercise unlocks all the cognitive benefits you need to manage your ADHD symptoms throughout the rest of the day. Morning exercise, in this way, is preferable to that of the evening, which may keep you awake and wired when you're supposed to be winding down to sleep. Even research has shown the advantage morning workouts have for ADHD.

EXERCISE INTENSITY

Many studies have shown the importance of intensity over quantity of exercise. Again, a 15-minute high-intensity exercise session can give you similar benefits to a 45 -minute low-intensity cardio session. It can also boost your overall fitness and endurance faster than steady-state aerobics.[10]

When it comes to ADHD, the literature is a bit divided. For children with ADHD, high-intensity exercise, in certain forms, may negatively impact mood fluctuations and behavior over time, according to one study. However, more research is needed.

Generally, high-intensity exercise is beneficial for adults' overall well-being, mood, and better behavioral control.

The truth lies in the middle; moderate exercise is the optimal choice for adults with ADHD. It is a perfect balance, between intense and mundane but not so excitatory that it increases risk-taking or impulsivity (as extreme sports may do). But I still advocate a few sessions of HIIT per week for the excellent benefits.

From personal experience, I can tell you that sports and exercise have been the most positive influences in my life. Had I not been able to get outside in nature and perform a variety of sports, my life would have been very different. I am grateful for not only the benefits of exercise on my total well-being and also the adventures I have been able to do as a result. I cannot give enough praise for the amazing benefits that exercise has done for my mental clarity. Now, make your own plan, get going and reap the rewards of exercise for yourself, you will thank me later!

Many of us with excess energy like to go-go-go, and exercise can be just the right type of catharsis to let out all that pent-up energy. However, the brain and body need rest and the right type. In the next chapter, we'll explore the importance of managing a sleep schedule conducive to thriving with ADHD.

～

"Physical fitness is not only one of the most important keys to a healthy body, it is the basis of dynamic and creative intellectual activity." —John F. Kennedy

Chapter 3

The Power Of Sleep

S leep- it's essential for brain and physical health. Do not underestimate the power of a great night's sleep. When you start letting your sleep hygiene slip, it slowly creeps up on your mental clarity and ability to make sound decisions.

While important for everyone, sleep is especially crucial for people with ADHD. With the many responsibilities that modern life demands from us during the day, sleep is often the only true rest our body gets. And most of us don't even get that small pleasure. Millions of Americans are sleep-deprived, and those with ADHD can take the brunt of their maladaptive sleeping patterns. Ensuring that you sleep well is a mandatory pillar of our holistic approach to improving ADHD symptoms.

That said, it's not as simple as falling onto your feather-soft mattress and snoozing immediately. While sleep is a biological need that our bodies know how to do naturally, somehow, we've managed to skew even that with some common bad habits.

. . .

First off, it's important to understand how sleep affects ADHD and the pitfalls or struggles for which we may be at risk.

OUR VULNERABILITY TO SLEEP ISSUES

Sleep can affect just about any condition. Because it dictates the well-being of your brain, it greatly impacts the course of your ADHD symptoms throughout the day. Moreover, ADHD itself can affect your sleep quality negatively. Adults with ADHD are more susceptible to various sleep issues due to both neurological and behavioral issues. Neurologically, the brain chemistry of a person with ADHD leads to difficulty falling asleep and staying asleep since so many hormones and neuro-transmitters are involved in sleep (i.e., dopamine, serotonin, cortisol, noradrenaline, etc.)

WHAT IS THE RELATIONSHIP BETWEEN ADHD AND SLEEP?

While the relationship between ADHD and sleep is not linear (meaning it isn't straightforward), it certainly is evident in the scientific literature. Clearly, at least 25 - 50% of people with ADHD suffer some type of sleep malady.[1] Some issues include insomnia, restless sleep, breathing issues (like sleep apnea), difficulty waking up in the morning, and more.

. . .

The connection is not only highly complex but also cyclical. ADHD and sleep have a circular relationship in which ADHD contributes to bad sleep, which worsens ADHD symptoms. Direct causes are not clear, but many experts point to the role of the body's circadian rhythm. This internal clock that biologically tells us when to sleep and wake up can be delayed in people with ADHD. One study about childhood-onset ADHD proposes that about 75 % of ADHD adults have this same delay of physiological differences concerning body temperature and melatonin secretion compared to neurotypical adults.[2] Even without evening distractions, many adults with ADHD naturally fall asleep an hour and a half later than others.

Now, let's throw the behavioral and psychological aspects of ADHD into the mix. At this point, you already know the struggle with ceasing the flow of thoughts and ideas at night, especially if you're going through a period of hyper-fixation on a subject or project. The body can remain fidgety and restless, leading to a repetitive movement to dispel the extra energy. People with ADHD also are prone to anxiety, which can be the cherry on top. A full night's sleep can feel like a dream, and getting through your responsibilities during the day can require more effort. A night of replaying your day's conversations and emotions can be exhausting, preventing deep sleep.

When starting your holistic journey, you must simultaneously address your sleep problems and ADHD. The two are so intrinsically intertwined that you can't prioritize one over the other. Otherwise, you may be spinning your wheels.

Chapter 3

ADHD AND SLEEP IN ADULTS

Even without ADHD, adults today are dealing with widespread sleep deprivation. Let's discuss the specific sleep ailments that can plague adults with ADHD. (Brues 2022):

Struggle with attention during the day? Maybe your sleep needs a tune-up.

Common sleep disorders:

- Insomnia (hard to fall asleep or stay asleep)
- RLS = restlessness; twitch or shake legs and/or arms during the night
- Narcolepsy = daytime sleepiness, during driving or socializing
- Circadian rhythm sleep disorders – a person's natural daily sleep cycles are disrupted
- Negative impact on mood, judgment, productivity, social life, etc.

POTENTIAL CAUSES FOR SLEEP PROBLEMS

Most of us with ADHD are not lucky when it comes to sleep. Only about 1 in every 5 adults with ADHD can get good sleep. Well, good for them! For the rest of us, we can struggle with long-term sleep deprivation or inconsistent sleep patterns that can lead to negative consequences later in life. Even in the short term, we can struggle with physical ailments and mood instability.

For the most part, sleep problems are correlated with ADHD. The causes for many of them may be linked with common ADHD-related aspects or behaviors. The following are some possible causes of sleep problems.

ADHD MEDICATION: Stimulants can act similarly to caffeine, which, of course, can mess with our sleep. This is particularly due to interaction with even small amounts of caffeine in other foods like tea, coffee, or chocolate. As for non-stimulant medication, a frequent side effect is drowsiness directly after taking it, which can lead to wakefulness at bedtime.

CAFFEINE AND ALCOHOL: Caffeine is one of the biggest destroyers of a healthy sleep schedule. Taking coffee or a soda as an afternoon pick-me-up can affect the body even hours after-ward, affecting your ability to fall asleep easily. As for alcohol, it can be a helpful "sleep-aid"— one I don't necessarily recom-mend—but it doesn't work well if you want to stay asleep. Often, people will have a disturbed, fitful sleep after a night of drinking, not to mention the inevitable hangover and late mornings.

ELECTRONICS: Phones have become the bane of healthy sleep. Watching television late into the night or scrolling your phone are not the best ways to drift into a peaceful sleep. More likely, they fill your brain with an immense amount of informa-tion and stimulation that can keep it working even after falling asleep. The distraction factor and addictive quality of electronics can keep you glued to them for longer than you intended. Playing a casual game in bed can turn into an hour of social media and another hour of aimless video-watching. Suddenly, it's one in the morning, and you're still wide awake.

ASSOCIATED DISORDERS & CONDITIONS

Let's talk a bit more about some of the sleep disorders we mentioned previously.

- **Circadian rhythm disorders:** Circadian rhythm is the 24-hour sleep-wake cycle that tends to be guided by the natural course of day and night. Sunrise supposedly prompts the body to wake up and sun down to get ready to sleep.[3] If you struggle with a circadian rhythm sleep disorder, your natural sleep cycles are disrupted for some reason or another.
- **Breathing disorders:** Breathing disorders are conditions that affect sleep and consist of everything from sleep apnea to snoring.[4]
- **Restless legs Syndrome**: This is the constant urge to continually move, twitch, wiggle, and shake at night without your conscious awareness, leading to difficulty falling asleep. It is common among both children and adults. RLS can be very disruptive and uncomfortable due to the prickling need in the legs to keep moving them. This condition is said to be related to the ADHD-dopamine connection. Reduced dopamine levels can lead to involuntary muscle movements, and combined with the fact that dopamine is naturally lowest at the end of the day, it's bad news for you if you want to rest. A holistic hack

for this is taking a magnesium powder supplement, like *Calm,* right before bed.

HACKS TO IMPROVE SLEEP QUALITY

Remember when I said that you couldn't treat ADHD without treating your sleep issues? It's true. Even if you're taking medications and doing everything right, neglecting proper sleep hygiene and failing to address any sleep disorders will keep you going two steps forward and one step back.

I urge you to consider the following tips to add to your day for consistent healthy sleep:

SET A SLEEP SCHEDULE (AND STICK TO IT!)

A healthy sleep schedule is not to be underestimated. Create a bedtime and morning routine that helps you get out of bed. Research has found that the most important thing is to be consistent. No matter what times you choose, you MUST wake up at the same time every day, be it six in the morning or noon (if that works with your daily responsibilities).

Consistency is most important in one's health and sleep depth. Inconsistent timing can throw your circadian rhythm off, affecting your hormones, mood, and ADHD symptoms. Of course, we also want to go to bed simultaneously every night. To do that, you need to build habits that make you successful in this regard. I like to pretend I'm going to sleep an hour earlier to give myself buffer time to draw away from whatever is grabbing my focus.

LIMIT SCREEN TIME

One of the biggest problems with screen time is exposure to blue light, which can throw your body off when it comes to sleep. Biologically, light (and lack of it) gives the signal to sleep or wake up. Blue light special blocks melatonin, which is what lulls you into a restful sleep. Right before bed, using screens, be it your smartphone, laptop, or television can delay sleep. The trick is to limit your screen time in the evening. I recommend stopping all electronic use an hour before your bedtime. If you must work late, use blue-light filtering glasses and computer programs like Flux the add a light filter to your screen after sunset.

INCREASE EXERCISE

As discussed in the previous chapter, exercise can work wonders for your sleep quality. All humans are supposed to move to use the energy they have. If you are feeling restless and alert at night, you have a lot of pent-up physical energy you aren't using during the middle of the day. You can test this on yourself by doing a long two-hour workout, bike, or hike and noting how well you sleep that night.

AVOID SUBSTANCES (CAFFEINE AND ALCOHOL)

Using caffeine and alcohol, especially in the evening, may not delay your sleep, but it can lead to shallow, fitful sleep, in which you can remain asleep. Avoid caffeine after 2:00 in the afternoon, and try to keep away from alcohol altogether.

SET YOUR BEDROOM UP FOR SUCCESS

Your bedroom should be a relaxing haven, not a disorganized war room. Ensure that your bed is clear, your screens are far away, and your bedside furniture is clear of distractions and clutter. Try to make your bed as comfortable and inviting as possible, with an abundance of pillows, throws, and a nice comforter. Some extra items can enhance the ambiance: a humidifier, scented candles, and your favorite book. Turn down the temperature since our bodies sleep in colder environments, between 60-67 degrees Fahrenheit. (Pacheco 2022)

WEIGHTED BALL BLANKET

Weighted blankets are an unusual hack that might boost your sleep quality. The blanket may weigh anywhere from 10 to 20 pounds and puts pleasant pressure on your body, which actually triggers serotonin in the brain. Serotonin is known to improve mood, sleep, and overall health.

Chapter 3

LISTEN TO AN AUDIOBOOK OR RELAXING MUSIC

If you need something to ground you from your distracting thoughts, an audiobook or music might be a good option to wind down. These activities aren't too stimulating, so long as the music is relaxing, like some Mozart or Vivaldi, or some Low-fi spa music. A plethora of sleep music tracks exists online for free listening. Half the reason why this tip works is that it pairs an enjoyable activity with sleep, making you more eager to jump into bed if you have something to look forward to. At the same time, they gradually relax you into sleep.

READ

Depending on your preference, reading a book or listening to an audiobook to help you relax and wind down. If you are the type of person who can't put an exciting book down until you find out what happens, rereading a book dear to you might be a better option. In general, though, reading is a preferred option over scrolling on social media, which can drag you down an endless descent into a rabbit hole. I have taken to keeping my phone out of the bedroom altogether. This also forces me to get out of bed, to turn off my alarm in the morning.

PLAY WHITE NOISE

White noise is underestimated as an ADHD tactic. Some people with ADHD claim that as soon as they listen to white noise, they finally feel relief from their ongoing internal chatter. It can help one focus on a task for an extended period and clear one's mind when trying to work through a project. White noise also blocks distracting factors in your environment.

People who have never struggled with getting a good night's sleep may take it for granted. However, the truth is that sleep is mainly underrated in today's fast-paced world. Society glamorizes sheer hard work and grit and looks down on resting your body and mind. Couple that with the fact that ADHD can make it even more difficult to sleep well, and you've got a recipe for disaster. Thus, creating an individually-tailored strategy is essential—it's the foundation for a healthy mind and spirit, which we will jump into in Parts II and III.

∼

"A good laugh and a long sleep are the two best cures for anything." —Irish Proverb

Part Two

THE MIND

Chapter 4

The Modern Mind

Our minds are much more powerful than we can comprehend. There is so much potential for good and bad depending on what information we consume and how we choose to think and believe, be it positive or negative. The mind is just as important, if not more so, as taking care of your body.

While ADHD can sometimes feel out of our control, your mind is always yours. Even in the wild, overgrown jungle of your imagination and the racing thoughts and ideas that ADHD can produce, those thoughts are still yours to command. After all, your mind is the origin of all action. Taming your mind to work for you, despite ADHD, requires knowing your focus.

Chapter 4

TECHNOLOGY AND THE BRAIN

The prevalence of technology and media in our modern life has created a stream of never-ending information, images, and distractions. It can be more than anyone can handle, especially if it's not managed wisely and intentionally.

Most of us have a technology and media addiction and now live in a society where we are all becoming programmed for shorter attention spans. Watch a group of millennials out to dinner; they are all on their cell phones, not being present with each other. I even have a photo of my 80- year-old parents both hyperfocused on their cell phones during a visit.

It takes conscious effort to be present; to engage with the people you are with, the task you are doing, and to be clear about your daily intentions. Recognizing your shortcomings, i.e., "I'm addicted to checking my phone, social media or online shopping," is a start to overcoming bad habits and inattention. It is amazing how much time we all waste on our phones each day, time that could be better spent harnessing our ADHD superpowers. I turn my phone off and put it in a drawer during work periods because, like potato chips, I can't be trusted if it's in sight.

SETTING GOALS

With a plethora of incoming information and daily task to accomplish, goal setting is the first step to grounding your mind. Goals are our written desires and actions to achieve a specific outcome. They are like signs along the road, indicating you arrived at a place on the map you wanted to go. Intentions are your thoughts and attitudes about the present moment and your relationship with people and the environment. Think of an intention as the journey experience and the goal as the destination or finish line.

We need both skills, but with ADHD, it is essential to learn to set goals. Do not be too hard on yourself if you do not achieve your goals; plans can change. Maybe your journey takes you in a different direction, and as Robert Frost says, "I took the road less traveled, and that has made all the difference." Setting goals gives you a basis to start creating a strategy. Goal setting is a skilled behavior that anyone can learn and excel at.

Let's examine the types of goals you can set; then, we'll discuss common problems ADHD adults may have with goal-setting.

TYPE OF GOALS

What many people don't know is the *right* way to set goals. It can seem simple — think about what you want in life, right? In reality, it's important to make the right kind of goals. We can make several types of goals, including learning goals, perfor-mance goals, and short-term and long-term goals.[1]

LEARNING GOALS

Is there any new skill or field you want to master? A learning goal is an aspiration to immerse yourself in a subject, be it astro-physics or salsa dancing. With learning goals, there is the measure of how much you have accomplished by the hours you put in and the new knowledge you now hold. You could also give a lecture or perform a dance.

PERFORMANCE GOALS

Performance goals are often based on your learning goals, but take it to the next step: practice. This can be challenging to do with ADHD, largely due to our inability to manage tasks prop-erly. It can feel like a huge task; if we can't do it well, we "fail." It doesn't help that many of us are perfectionists. When laying out performance goals, we will soon find out that breaking a big task into smaller, realistic pieces works best.

SHORT-TERM VS. LONG-TERM GOALS

Differentiating your goals by their potential duration is critical since ADHD can sometimes make it difficult to grasp big, far-away milestones.

. . .

Short-term goals are essential for boosting morale and giving you a hit of dopamine along the way to your greater-purpose goals. Such goals can be daily, weekly, or monthly and feed the ADHD brain's love of instant gratification. Regularly, enjoying small wins builds your patience for the more rewarding gratification you are delaying.

Long-term goals are the major milestones that can take months, even years, to reach. They involve many steps and complexities but also provide the biggest reward. These are our aspirations, like getting a degree, writing a book, winning a local sports competition, or running a marathon. Because they are so far off in the future, the impulsive part of yourself may struggle to remember to stick to your intentions in the present. Without the right organizational skills, we may lack the mental discipline to see long-term goals through.

The good thing is that ADHD can give you the power to take you to the finish line. With the bonus of creativity and the unique ability to hyperfocus, ADHD adults can make the most of their goals, especially when they are passionate about them. See! Channeled ADHD characteristics can indeed become superpowers.

WHY WE STRUGGLE WITH GOALS

Why does ADHD make us more prone to struggle to meet goals, even those we care about most? Most of it is due to how our dopamine-driven reward center works. Because of our naturally low dopamine levels, we need even more external (or internal) stimulation to prompt us to derive rewards from tasks that we deem mundane or tedious, even if they will help us in the long run.

Short-term gratification is more tempting since we struggle to see the bigger picture, the far-off future. The "now" moment is often more interesting and stimulating than a vague concept. It's also why many of us work best under pressure — the urgency of a looming deadline gives us just enough stimulation to push us into working, despite the stress it causes. Because of less-developed executive functioning, we can have time blindness. Estimating how long a task will take or how much time has passed confuses us. Thus, setting up deadlines, scheduling time windows for daily tasks, and planning overall don't come naturally.

Finally, prioritizing is another hurdle. We often struggle to weigh a task's importance relative to others. Having too much on our plate can lead to overwhelm, avoidance, or inefficient multitasking. Our emotions, moods, and level of stimulation act on how we judge a task, making us more prone to impulsive choices.[2]

Fortunately, all of these struggles are tied to skills we can work on if we do so correctly. That starts with how you choose your goals.

WHAT GOOD GOALS LOOK LIKE

I'm going, to be honest here: Not all goals are good. Sure, you may have positive intentions, but sometimes, if you find yourself not living up to your expectations, your goals might be the problem. Luckily, there is a way to create strategic goals that work for you and provide you with a strategic basis.

According to the Substance Abuse and Mental Health Services Administration, a good goal is a SMART goal– specific, measured, achievable, relevant, and time-based.[3]

- 1. **Specific**: What exactly are your goals, and what actions (specific) will you take to complete them? For example, rather than be an excellent piano artist, your goal is to play piano for a set amount of time a day. The more specific it is, the more measurable the goal is, and the more accomplished you will feel when you complete each milestone.
- 2. **Measured**: Always quantify your goal so that you can better meet them, rather than leave it open, which can lead to doing too much one day and slacking off the next. Moreover, it gives you a more concrete focus, i.e. writing a 60k-word novel.
- 3. **Achievable**: Sometimes, our ADHD minds can imagine high aspirations for ourselves — so high that we fall far after failing to reach them in real life. Avoid disappointment by creating realistic goals based on your existing likes, dislikes, strengths, and weaknesses. If you get winded walking up three

stories, running a marathon after only a month of preparation might be far-fetched.

- 4. **Relevant**: If you aren't passionate about your goal, it will be much more difficult to stick to it. This usually happens if you follow someone's well-meaning advice that doesn't necessarily resonate with you (i.e. a fad diet or new fitness craze). Trust me, if you have ADHD, choosing a goal most relevant to your truth is essential and more likely to be successful.

- 5. **Time-based**: Keeping your goal timeline open can be tricky because it may lead to procrastination. Instead, set an ultimate deadline for your goal so you can stay on track and assess your progress more properly.

TIPS TO IMPROVE YOUR GOALS

Part of goal setting is to have at least an inkling of an idea as to where to start. Along with setting SMART goals, there are some additional foundational keys to creating effective goals. The following tips allow you to transform your goal into a series of steps *and* stick to the journey.

SET MEANINGFUL GOALS

A truly smart goal resonates. I can show you how to choose goals that are meaningful to you and make universally important goals more personal. It also needs a perfect balance between passion and attainability.

When setting meaningful goals, a good exercise is to write them out and meditate on *why* you want to do them. This is your purpose. Sometimes the *why* may come easy to you; other times, it may require some thinking. Perhaps you'll come to the conclusion that you don't care much about the goal at all. Regardless, the meaningful purpose boosts your attachment to the goal and increases motivation. Finally, think of a single, simple step that can give you the momentum you need; a small task you can do daily.

BREAK GOALS DOWN INTO STEPS

ADHD can make it challenging to take a goal and create a plan, prioritize tasks, and set deadlines. In the past, this made me prone to avoidance because, in my head, the goal just felt so big and vague that I didn't know where to start. To avoid the pitfall of being overwhelmed by a huge goal, you must make your goal as easy as possible by breaking it up into smaller, digestible tasks.

Some people call this technique 'chunking.' This is the act of cutting a big, long-term task into smaller, daily, or weekly subtasks. First, it helps to consider the length of time your goal might take. Since many of us have time blindness, simply google the average time your specific goal may take to give you a ballpark estimate. Then, list all the subtasks needed to meet your goal. So if you want

59

to learn a language, you might commit to an hour of reading/writing practice every other day and listening/speaking practice on the odd days. Based on the estimated timeline, spread the subtasks out, and set potential milestone dates to track your progress. For instance, if you're following a language learning textbook, you might commit to completing four units in one month.

Finally, do not allow the allure of perfectionism to lure you into its trap. If you miss a day or a subtask, think about the larger picture: you still accomplished your subtasks on the other six days of the week. Use positive self-talk to broaden your perspective. For instance, talk yourself out of guilt or disappointment for avoiding the tasks you need to do by reminding yourself of your purpose. Moreover, celebrate small wins, like making it through at least 15 minutes of practicing a language rather than an hour; if that's all you can push yourself to do. Like exercise and sleep, consistency wins again!

STRATEGIZE SELF-MOTIVATION

Many people say that self-discipline is more important than motivation. Perhaps this is true to an extent, but remember, we are dealing with a disorder in which controlling one's discipline is difficult, simply due to how our brain is wired. Neurotypical people can train their minds to build sheer willpower, but people with ADHD's dopamine deficiency find the reward system even harder to stick to — but as soon as you are genuinely interested in something, nothing can stop you. Thus, you must use motivation to your advantage, and that is something anyone can harness and increase. While motivation can seem vague and out of control, it is also a skill you can build.

. . .

Beware of the urge to avoid. Make procrastination your nemesis and identify what is truly important to you and what is not worthwhile (procrastinating). Build confidence with a growth mindset. Despite our many failures in life, we have just as many or more successes. Remember them often to build your sense of confidence and pump yourself up. Use self-talk once more, as much as you can, when you aren't feeling up to a task. Rather than guilt-trip yourself, which can do more damage, remind yourself repetitively of your purpose.[4]

HOW TO MEET YOUR GOALS WITHOUT DIFFICULTY: KEEP IT FUN AND ENJOYABLE

Another pitfall we with ADHD are at high risk for is devastating boredom. Sometimes, it's hard for us to stick to a path or goal because the process can quickly become tedious and lack the initial spark of interest. All the more important is to continually find ways to make your journey more enjoyable. Keeping things fresh and interesting is the best way to motivate you to continue meeting your goals.

One way to do this is to take regular breaks, maybe every 30 minutes, so that you don't run out of steam. Just 5 minutes of doing something you love can increase your energy meter and refresh your motivation to continue the task.

Chapter 4

REWARD YOURSELF

Feel like you can't wait to feel the reward of meeting your goal? Try this– pair a positive thing that you enjoy with the daily tasks you need to do. For instance, if you're learning a language, watch your favorite movies and TV shows in that language. Listen to a favorite audiobook or a dopamine-boosting playlist every time you go on a run.

People with ADHD thrive on instant gratification, so we may as well use that to our advantage. Rewarding ourselves in this way boosts morale and brings fun to any boring task. Over time, your brain may even associate the less pleasant activities you must do with that enjoyable thing and become rewarding in itself. I use my favorite podcast to stay focused while doing mundane tasks like cleaning bathrooms and floors.

Alternatively, you might reward yourself after every goal-related task you do. Perhaps you can go on an outing to a new place or a favorite; you may buy yourself something new, like a book, or try that new cafe downtown. The trick is to turn the stuff you would rather be doing all the time into precious rewards, increasing their value and giving you more reason to do the stuff you should.

REASSESS

What if your goal isn't going as planned? Sometimes, you may need to reflect and reassess your goal rather than spinning your wheels or giving up. Is it still important to you? Have your feelings about it changed? Is it taking longer and needs an extension on the deadline? Is it the plan or your expectations? Are you being impatient and a perfectionist about it? It helps to ask an outside observer for their point-of-view of your progress.

It's okay to reassess. That's life, and it's normal to make changes. Sometimes being too stringent on one path or one way of doing things can be more limiting than beneficial, and it's not how we all work. Remain flexible.

Once you've set up goals that tick all the boxes, it's time to move on to structuring your days around them, which we'll discuss in the next chapter.

$\sim$

"She knew the power of her mind,
so programmed it for success." — Carrie Green

Chapter 5

Structuring Your Days

I have always been a calendar-keeping, note-taking, and post-it-making machine. As a kid, I was fascinated with stationery stores, colored pens, and organizational calendars. Writing EVERYTHING down is essential to my success and has helped me immensely. If I do nothing else, I will scribble out a 'to-do' list each day. Part of my incessant brain chatter comes in the form of reminding myself what needs to be done. Once down on paper, it's like cleaning house in your mind. Putting it down on paper is better than having nagging thoughts annoy you day and night. If you tend to worry and fret as you fall asleep, a brain dump into a journal is a great solution. There are many ways to bring structure to our flying thoughts, but it is best to devise a real plan.

Regarding mental hacks for improving ADHD, boosting our executive function should be our target. One way to do that is by learning critical organization techniques, like structuring your daily life. Having a schedule and practicing the art of following is a habit that anyone can build and it's one that can unlock a wealth of advantages for your ADHD brain.

Not only does organizing your time and structuring your day keeps you focused on priority tasks, but also intersects your goals with their execution.

THE IMPORTANCE OF STRUCTURE FOR ADHD

Did you know that one of the best ways to improve a child's ADHD symptoms is to give them a structured daily schedule? Guess what — it's the same case with adults. Routine is healthy for anyone by improving depression, time management, anxiety, organization, and overall personal success. It gives you more control over your life. That's exactly what we need to reign in our ADHD symptoms.

For those with ADHD, a set daily structure offers a predictable foundation of control that offsets our whims and attention's often unpredictable, ever-shifting nature. Just as young children with ADHD can train themselves to regulate their emotions and behaviors when they know what will happen next in the day, adults can also use structure to improve self-control. It helps by keeping environmental and contextual factors stable.

For instance, if you get into the habit that every day at 10 AM after breakfast, you take a walk and then, on the way back, run errands (i.e., pick up any needed groceries or supplies, visit the post office, etc.), you will come to expect it. It becomes automatic, like clockwork. It becomes little effort to force yourself to go out and fulfill your errands and get things you may need when you don't feel like it. In other words, your behavior begins to match environmental cues rather than be controlled by unpredictable feelings throughout the day. In that way, this reduces any stress you might have when starting a task you don't necessarily want to do or that you dread completing.

Knowing what to expect each day counters any negative effects of unmanaged impulsivity. You're less likely to follow what you feel like doing, which may not always be conducive to what you should do. It also keeps you focused on your goals by inserting the daily tasks you must do to meet those long-term goals. That interplay between expectations and a stable, predictable environment creates the most optimal situations for you to complete your responsibilities successfully.

If you are the more anxious type regarding ADHD, structure alleviates that by offering a bubble of clarity and security. In summary, here are the benefits you can hope to get from managing your day:

- Predictability of the day's structure allows for better behavioral control.
- Less resistance to dreaded tasks.
- Reduced stress by setting up lists and expectations.
- Reduced disorganization combats forgetfulness and prevents being late or missing deadlines.
- A strong foundation for building habits that make you more productive with ADHD.

TIPS TO CREATE DAILY STRUCTURE

When structuring your weekday, you need to equip yourself with some useful tips, so you don't barrel into the task unprepared.

CREATE A SCHEDULE AHEAD OF TIME

You need to plan ahead. Remember that planning is a skill that you can become stronger at. Often, we may underestimate the difficulty of planning, but the truth is, it's hard. Acting like it's an easy thing you can do last minute or at the beginning of your day is only setting yourself up for failure. I had to accept that if I wanted to succeed, planning had to become a necessary ritual in my life— like brushing my teeth or taking a shower.

I learned to create a general weekly schedule every Sunday and more detailed day schedules every night for the next day, which has been a game changer!

If you have trouble filtering through what you need to do, it's time to practice prioritization. First, when you sit down to plan, during whatever time you choose (make sure it's a time in which you're alert and focused rather than sluggish and ready to wind down), make a list of every task on your mind. You're essentially brain-dumping here.

Next, highlight the necessary obligations that you cannot get out of (events, recurrent errands or tasks, deadlines, etc.), and then last your personal, goal-focused tasks you intend to accomplish the coming week. Any other flighty ideas or sudden desires can be left at the bottom of the prioritization list. Now, fit those tasks into your weekly/daily schedule using the time-blocking technique, you can use a spreadsheet program if it works for you. This helps you realistically fill your day while leaving time for meals, breaks, and morning and night routines.

You'll find that you can't do nearly as much as you think or wish you could. However, you can better prepare yourself to do what you must, which is more than you would have otherwise been able to get through without a structure.

BREAK IT DOWN INTO SIMPLE TASKS

As mentioned earlier, when a significant task is too overwhelming, it becomes an intimidating dark cloud following you everywhere. You have to deal with it eventually, but it's like vapor that your hands can't get a hold of. There's no practical way for you to tackle it because it's just a vague construct too large to get under control. When this is the case, the solution is to break it down into smaller units, as small as you can possibly make them so that they are ridiculously easy to tackle. Take it a step further by blocking time into smaller chunks rather than hour-long stretches. For instance, each subtask can take up to 25 minutes at a time. This makes it easier than visualizing the estimated duration of your goal completion.

USE TIMERS AND REMINDERS

Remember that having a schedule laid out may not be enough. You need to exercise your discipline and put a little bit of pressure on your ADHD senses to stick to your schedule as best as possible. Tools like a timer or alarm clock can take a major weight off your shoulders because they prevent procrastinating and keep your efforts contained within the desired time that you allotted. After all, work "expands to fill the time" given for its completion, according to Parkinson's Law. Having a limit and environmental constraint keeps you on task.

BUILD ON IT AND ADJUST AS YOU GO

Perfectionism is not the goal. Your schedule doesn't have to be perfect, and you don't need to follow it exactly for it to greatly benefit your life and habits. The only thing we want to avoid is giving up and throwing away the schedule after we don't meet our high expectations the first few times.

This is where I went wrong when I was first trying out solutions. I thought that planning just "wasn't my thing." That isn't true at all. Having a growth mindset allows you to see time management as a skill, not an ingrained talent or trait we are born with. If you can follow your plan for one week, that's progress! The next goal is two days a week. Then three. It becomes a game in which you can clearly see how much your skills are improving, so keep trying, rework your schedule as you go, and don't quit. Don't put too much pressure on yourself; even if you try a simple form of the above, you will be surprised by your progress.

WHAT A GOOD SCHEDULE INCLUDES

You will eventually need to build a schedule as you progress, and it will teach you about your energy fluctuations throughout the day. We think that creating a schedule doesn't require much critical thought; just make a to-do list and complete the list. Simple! We forget to take into consideration unpredictable moods or energy dips.

When planning, consider what you are feeling, at least cognitively. For instance, consider how you might be feeling before lunch (low blood sugar, tired, low energy, irritable), or at night (tired, sleepy, grumpy), when you're planning to do that project you've been procrastinating.[1]

Ultra-rhythm is the cycle of energy lows and highs your body undergoes through the day. Since it's so individual, I had to focus my attention in order to observe my patterns and understand how factors like food, coffee, sleep, and activity affect them. The better you know yourself and your body, the better you can plan your day around your states, with better emotional empathy and compassion.

A GOOD SCHEDULE INCLUDES THE FOLLOWING:

- 1. Morning routine

- 2. Recurrent tasks
- 3. Appointments and obligations
- 4. Tasks that serve the goals you have set
- 5. Breaks and transitions
- 6. Evening routine

There are other important things to include that we forget amid our responsibilities. Make sure you prioritize the following tasks in your schedule and make time for them so you don't skimp out on taking care of yourself.

- Time to Eat
- Time to Exercise
- Time to Sleep
- Time for Self-Care

When filling in your schedule, you will find that you must let go of a few tasks you may have wanted to do or felt the need to do. This is normal. One of the great benefits of making schedules is realizing how much time you have in the day. This leads to more realistic planning and less disappointment.

USING A PLANNER

Many people avoid using a planner before even trying, and it tends to be these same people who need it the most. Time management can be a challenging skill, but it's one that we can all learn. Most of the time, it's a matter of not knowing how to build these time management skills.2 Strengthening organizational skills and working memory, which gives you the power to hold new knowledge while using it simultaneously, is essential for executive functioning.

To improve these skills, having a planner and using it consistently can help. The advantages are numerous: Firstly, it gives you a layout to set up the daily structure you need to manage your days. Many planners are annual, so you can plan for the short-term while stabilizing your long-term goals in the later pages rather than floating somewhere in your brain. Another pro is that it helps you remember responsibilities and errands, a major ADHD shortcoming. A planner allows you to organize all events, family obligations, billing dates, children's school events, etc.

A planner isn't just a calendar but a to-do list with space for notes. Try a time block planner that breaks up the day into hours and allows you to visualize how long each task will take.

Your planner of choice can be paper or electronic, like one of the many time management apps available, which you can bring up on your phone or laptop whenever and wherever. I prefer a physical book I can take with me anywhere (anything can be portable if you make a conscious effort!). Technology is too much for me. I get lost on my phone. In contrast, a book in front of me offers visibility and the ability to jot things down quickly as they come to me. I use it for everything from workouts, walks, work-related tasks, family events, reminders, and random ideas that come to me that I just need to unload or I'll forget.

. . .

Being a visual person, I find it best to see the entire month all at once. Try and see what works best for you, but I recommend you don't go without a planner, or you will risk having to make spontaneous decisions and forgetting obligations. I take a photo of my paper calendar and voila- it's electronic! HAA!

Again implementing any of these strategies can go a long way to helping you organize the cluttering thoughts of your mind and setting you up for more success! Structuring time is invaluable for us with ADHD. In the next chapter, we're moving to organize your environment to best suit your lifestyle.

∽

"A goal without a plan is just a wish."
—Antoine de Saint-Exupéry.

Chapter 6

Structuring Your Environment

Nothing stresses out an ADHD mind like clutter and a chaotic environment. Cluttered space, cluttered mind. While I'm not perfect regarding my mess, I do try to clean, organize and eliminate things that no longer serve me so I can find calm in my environment. My friend's mother once told her kids to make their beds every day, to set you on a positive path. I do it and it actually works!

We have moved frequently over the years and have used it as an opportunity to pare our 'stuff' down. We created a more minimalist environment in our new home that has that contributes to a clear and peaceful mind.

When children are diagnosed with ADHD, classroom recommendations exist to support them in their education. Most of these recommendations involve manipulating the physical space around the ADHD student(s) to promote their success rather than hinder them. Adults are no different, especially with

ADHD. Just as these techniques work for children at school, they also make a huge difference in our ADHD symptoms in our home and work environments.

WHAT WE CAN LEARN FROM THE CLASSROOM EXPERIENCE

Let's discuss the classroom experience for ADHD kids and what we can learn form it. The best classroom environment for children includes several elements: clear rules and guidelines, positive reinforcement; an overall calm air; flexibility; supportiveness; consistency, and structured physical space.

Structure is important for children and adults with ADHD because it offers predictability and organization that otherwise is not possible in the mind of the person with ADHD. A disorganized environment will lead to distractions, fighting for the divided attention of the person with ADHD. Structures reinforced by the environment allow children to feel more secure and stabilized because they know what to expect, making their behaviors easier to manage. It is even more important in the work environment.

While children, in general, can benefit from structure and routine, kids with ADHD need it even more. If we leave them in an unstructured environment, they are unable to build critical life skills. For children with ADHD, this gives the right expectations. That way, they can better prepare to regulate themselves. In addition, keeping the structure of the class and the direction of the teacher consistent is essential so that children can essentially undergo in-life behavioral therapy where their brain forms associations between environmental factors and the right way to act.[1]

WHAT YOUR ENVIRONMENT MUST REFLECT

Adult ADHD, can negatively impact work performance. Adults with undiagnosed ADHD won't be able to figure out what's wrong with them, and they may come off as lazy or unmotivated, affecting their financial stability, career goals, and self-esteem. Just like the classroom environment, you have to set your work space up for success.

DEALING WITH DISTRACTIONS

Just like in a classroom, the first thing you must change in your environment is reducing distractions in any way possible. When you're at work, you might have a crowded, noisy environment that can dampen your mental clarity. With ADHD, you struggle with filtering distractions, barely breaking through your coworkers' focus. One helpful thing that I do is listen to "alpha brain wave music for study" on YouTube with earbuds to drown out ambient noise and distractions.

MANAGING A SHORT ATTENTION SPAN

Having a short attention span can wreak havoc on your work life. Productivity can take a hit since you're unable to maintain focus on your tasks long enough to get major work done. A simple project can take longer than usual, leading to stress, unhappy team members, and a displeased boss. This looks a lot like mind wandering, losing track of your thoughts, and being unable to listen at the key moments – all clear inattentive ADHD symptoms.

ORGANIZATION AND MEMORY

Some ways to keep up your organization levels in your workspace is to reduce all potential for you to miss a deadline or accidentally forget something crucial. It starts with building critical organizational habits like using a planner, taking notes of any information or direction you receive from supervisors, and keeping visual reminders of what you need to do.

Note-taking is your best friend, so accept it with welcome arms. Take notes of *everything*. Write down big work events, small tasks, and daily recurring tasks, and use an abundance of sticky notes.

Visuals checklists will help you keep up with longer-term projects. You can do this by having a large wall calendar or whiteboard on which you can put up post-it notes, draw visuals for tasks, or use colors to organize your schedule.

. . .

Of course, these organizational tips work in company-type situations (if you're working an office or desk job) and in a home environment if you work from the comfort of your house. That's a different conversation, and it requires just as much effort to keep up work-vs-home boundaries and stay focused despite being surrounded by the place where you prefer to relax and have fun.

COPING WITH HYPERACTIVITY

Although hyperactivity isn't seen externally in adults with ADHD, it still manifests in ways that can make us struggle more in a formal workplace. You might be familiar with the sense of edginess, which can worsen if you struggle with anxiety and stress at work. It can hold you back from relaxing enough to become wrapped up in a period of hyperfocus. Many people with ADHD can be restless in their job, feeling like it is a prison, making it much more unbearable to be in an office environment, and have had to find ways to cope and manage this.

A few ways to counter this internalized hyperactivity is to have many breaks. As many breaks as you possibly can within the limits of your workplace. By breaks, I mean you must get up and move around a little, shake your body, and refresh your brain. Visit the break room if there is one, say hi to your coworkers, and do a round on the workplace ground. Even if you're at home, it's important to schedule regular breaks to be bogged down by the same task or position for a long period of time. Some tools that can help with that, are standing desks or a large yoga ball.[2]

. . .

Even if you don't have any of these tools, there are ways to keep yourself stimulated, which is another reason why this restlessness occurs. Essentially, your brain does not produce enough dopamine and other feel-good neurotransmitters, leading to you feeling trapped and bored in your situation and needing to do something to save yourself. Many feel uncontrollably compelled to shake their leg, tap on the desk, play with a pen or rock their body back and forth. Often, there is pressure to stop these sorts of natural movements. I urge you to allow yourself to do these movements to provide sensory stimulation because they will help you feel more grounded and focused.

This is why fidget spinners and stress balls were made, and it has its roots in scientific literature. After all, we have decided to accept ourselves more and more now. One of the ways to do that is to stop masking if it is actually detrimental to us, or at least not as beneficial. Let yourself bounce, fidget, or chew on your pen; if it helps you channel some energy.

At least five or ten minutes of physical breaks let your body release the otherwise stuck energy within you. Even just talking with a person helps break up the monotony of the day. If your symptoms are especially severe, don't be afraid to ask your supervisor for more time during breaks or more time to finish your project.[3]

Chapter 6

DEALING WITH CLUTTER

With ADHD, the mess can be the norm. That's not to say we are messy as people — metaphorically, we just can't resist getting all the paint colors out on the table. Sometimes (or all the time), clutter is just inevitable, and we can't keep spending every few hours cleaning up after ourselves. At home, perhaps clutter isn't that big of a deal, and at work, there's just a little bit of haphazardly organized items and folders or files. How do you know if your clutter is a problem?

Is clutter keeping you from optimizing your day? Are you wasting too much time looking for lost items like those elusive car keys or an important document on a daily basis? If your clutter is literally an obstacle to functional living, then it's time to make a change. If you don't, the situation could evolve into something that affects others, like family members, friends, and even coworkers. Or it may be problematic in insidious ways. For instance, although you can generally find what you need in your surrounding chaos, you might not realize how distracting it really is for your overall performance.

To address your clutter, be it at home or at work, there are techniques to live with it better or structure your environment to be more minimal regarding distracting items: [4]

- Use boxes and containers for specific items
  Designated "other" drawers or containers.
- Wastebaskets in every room in which to discard
  unnecessary objects and papers

- Use magazine racks and bookshelves to store items in the meantime
- Take time out of your day to declutter (don't let it accumulate!)

__Try the following tools to help you manage your environment__: [5]

Alarm clock: Use an alarm clock or timer to time yourself doing organizational tasks or chores. This helps you be more conscious of time passing and avoid losing track of time. A good rule of thumb is keep it anytime between 15 -30 minutes at a time depending on how distracted you are feeling at the time.

Apple AirTags, Tile Pro, and Similar Finders: Who knew there was a way to keep those pesky car keys from getting lost every time you need to leave your house? A tool called a finder exists to alert you to where important items are so you never have to worry if you misplace them. It's a tracker that you attach to the object and it connects to a phone application that lets you know its location at all times. Apple AirTags and Tile Pro are some of the finder brands, but many other affordable brands are available on the market.

Post-it notes: I've already talked a little bit about post-it notes and I am passionate about their many functional uses, from reminding you of events and tasks you must do to creating lists that you can keep in sight. The ability to stick Post-it notes in your immediate surroundings is so valuable, keeping information top of mind and training your working memory. Did you know that it will continue to deteriorate exponentially if you don't give your working memory a little shake? The best way to improve your memory, despite ADHD, is to keep what you want to remember in front of you. And post-it notes are one great way to do this.

Setting up your environment in such a manner will surely improve your well-being from the get-go with smoother daily routines that will bring more calm to your life. Taking time to reflect and self-care will often prove more useful, as we glide into harnessing your spirit in the next chapter.

∽

"Clutter is nothing more than postponed decisions."
— Barbara Hemphill

Part Three

THE SPIRIT

Chapter 7

Breathing & Meditation

The pandemic was a turning point for me because it required me to stay put. I took that as an opportunity to turn inward and work on my personal goals. I started a yoga, meditation, and weightlifting routine each morning. The pandemic lockdown helped me to clear my head and understand my priorities. Everyone had to stay home—how liberating for an extravert! After lockdown, I no longer cared about social events or needing other's approval. I decided that we are all unique individuals and get to do life our unique way. I figured that one person's definition of success wasn't necessarily mine.

I now understand that fulfillment and joy in life come from accepting and loving yourself, just as you are. Realizing it is okay to just BE, not always achieving, is very liberating. I am more present, enjoying life, the time I spend here on earth with these wonderful people, and the beauty of nature surrounding us. I fully believe in manifesting and creating a life of happiness, and have purposely created a slower, more happy life of solitude in our mountain home with my spouse. Our visitors are the moose and elk that migrate through each morning and evening. This is a life we chose and worked hard to create.

Nurturing my spirit has become an amazing anchor for me in my struggles. Even though ADHD is a brain disorder, it impacts parts of the brain involved in your emotional response. As we all know, how we feel affects who we are consistently and how we behave. It has a huge influence on behavioral regulation in ADHD. Without taking care of this side of ourselves, our ADHD symptoms can run amok.

Ultimately, practical skills that help you in your everyday life are nothing without a healthy soul. In more down-to-earth terms, being emotionally and mentally stable and taking care of your psychological well-being is half the equation of managing your ADHD.

DEEP BREATHING

Everyone from health professionals, to mental health experts, and yoga teachers are promoting the importance of deep breathing. What's the big deal? We breathe every day. The truth is, we're not breathing in the correct way. We are not conscious of our breath enough to control our physiological and emotional state. When we're in high emotion, we tend to disconnect from our body, unaware of our rapid breathing, high heart rate, and overproduction of stress hormones.

WHAT IS DEEP BREATHING?

Deep breathing is a practice of consciously and deliberately, inhaling and exhaling as much breath as possible; it is a learned technique. Just because all humans can breathe doesn't mean a deep breathing session will come naturally the first time someone tries it. We'll go over the step-by-step way to breathe deeply more thoroughly later, but it generally involves belly or diaphragmatic breathing. Your diaphragm is right under the rib cage. You must fill up both your chest and abdomen, your stomach rising with every inhale. Above all, deep breathing is a slow, purposeful skill that can provide many advantages.

WHAT ARE THE BENEFITS OF DEEP BREATHING?

Where do I start with the advantages deep breathing can have in your life? It benefits your brain, emotional and mental health, physical health, and overall energy levels.[1]

MENTAL HEALTH

Deep breathing has several advantages for one's emotional state. The main benefit is its fantastic effects on stress and anxiety. Deep breathing works wonders to override your body's fight-or-flight system.

When stress triggers a flurry of adrenaline and cortisol, you can experience a high heart rate, increased blood pressure, rapid, shallow breathing, and so on. Deep breathing slows down our parasympathetic nervous system, providing that feeling of calm. This physiological response is activated by real and false stressors, like caffeine or something exciting. Triggering it too much can leave our body in a constant state of emergency state, leading to minimal time to relax and recover; mentally and physically. Sometimes, even if you feel mentally positive, if your body enters its fast-paced stress response physiologically, it can trick your brain into thinking you are in danger. The solution? Hijack the body by slowing it down with deep, controlled breaths. Anytime you feel overwhelmed, you can sit and force yourself into a state of relaxation through deep breathing; it's a free, healthy coping mechanism. I regularly use long deep breaths to get back to sleep and come back from a highly emotional state.

PHYSICAL HEALTH

Physical health is the most surprising benefit of deep breathing. For starters, deep breathing can immediately lower blood pressure. Because it lulls you into a more calm state with a slower, steadier heart rate, your blood vessels dilate or expand wider to allow more blood through, and thus lower blood pressure. That improved circulation allows nutrients and oxygen to reach organs more completely. As a result, your digestion can improve, which is further helped by the stress-relieving effects of deep breathing since your intestinal health is closely connected to stress.

Blood circulation also is tied to detoxification. When you breathe in, oxygen enters the bloodstream and organs, and breathing out expels the carbon monoxide in your body and other toxins. Failing to breathe properly means your body is not efficiently getting rid of built-up toxins and cellular waste, which aren't disposed of through the bladder and bowels. As a result, we can lose energy because our body tries to compensate for this by managing the waste on its own.

Finally, constructing a deep breathing practice daily can eventually improve your posture. Deep breathing uses muscles you aren't used to using, forcing your abdomen, back, and chest muscles to get stronger to encourage more oxygen input. As a result, your posture inevitably straightens out.

ENERGY

Improved blood circulation leads to a greater volume of oxygen circulating in the blood, fueling the body's cell function and generating more energy. If you have ADHD, you might struggle with inconsistent energy levels. Forcing yourself to function daily and push through your behavioral impulses can be exhausting. Doing risky behavior like staying up late and working on something you procrastinated on can lead to a low-energy morning. Short deep breathing sessions throughout the day can be just the pick-me-up you need.

HOW TO DEEP BREATHE, THE RIGHT WAY

Yes, there is a right way to breathe.[2] Most people are so used to breathing from their chest that deep breathing can require a learning curve since it is breathing into the diaphragm. Follow the steps below for at least 10 minutes a day to unlock the benefits of deep breathing:

1. First, ensure you are comfortable, sitting in a quiet, distraction-free place or laying back on a soft surface. No matter what position you're in, put a hand over your diaphragm, which is located below your ribs and above your belly button. You can also place your other hand over your chest if you like more physical feedback. Take a normal breath and see how that feels.
2. Next, take the deepest breath you can. Breathe in through your nostrils, imagining air going down your airway, filling up your diaphragm like a balloon; the hand on your abdomen should rise.
3. Pause between the inhale and the exhale for only about a second.
4. Then, release your breath into a long, slow, drawn-out exhale. Your diaphragm should contract, and the hand on your abdomen will lower.
5. Maintain a stable rhythm, focusing on each deep breath until you can almost do it automatically. To keep engaged by the exercise, visualize positive energy entering your body with every inhale and negative energy and stress leaving with every exhale.

If you don't have time to spare for a full-on breathing session, remember to pause for at least 2- 5 minutes throughout your day and do some deep breathing. The more you do it, the easier it becomes, and you can even insert it as one of your frequent breaks between work or home tasks.

. . .

DAILY MEDITATION

Mindfulness is an important skill we must build, even if ADHD can make us miss out on being in tune with the details around us. We learned about deep breathing, which proves to be important in mindfulness meditation; allows you to come back to the moment, consider it practice for reigning in your attention, and improving your focusing muscles.

Like breathing's plethora of benefits, meditation also helps reduce mental health symptoms like depression and anxiety. Meditation improves overall mood, making you more positive immediately afterward and stabilizing our minds in the long run. Meditation also helps you connect more with yourself. Meditation forces you to stay still, sit with your mind, be more intentional about your life and actions, and sift through the flurry of thoughts that race through your mind all day.

One way to be more mindful daily is to establish a meditation practice. Just 10-15 minutes a day can lead to a domino effect of benefits in our lives.[3]

BENEFITS OF MEDITATION FOR PEOPLE WITH ADHD

One benefit of meditation for people with ADHD is that it can counteract our inability to chill in one position for longer than a few minutes at a time. In other words, it combats restlessness.

You are essentially training your body to better control itself. Besides that, meditation has many benefits throughout your day, like increasing your productivity, improving your overall mood and emotional regulation skills, and reducing stress. Why do we gain all these benefits – just by sitting and doing nothing for a quarter of an hour? Meditation forces you to gradually gain control of your mind by being more aware of it and observing it, which may be the switch many people need to snap back into the moment from anxiety. Secondly, it helps by allowing the mind to truly rest from the storm that life sends every day. It is possible to train yourself to just BE without any expectations.

Since meditation increases your overall awareness, it also reduces the severity of things like food addiction and sleep issues. One thing to keep in mind is that you won't become a meditation guru overnight. It's easy to try it a couple of times and then think it's not working because you keep thinking about whatever random topics are buzzing through your mind. It's understandable to question if it's working when you don't yet see the promised benefits after a few days or weeks. But trust me, they'll come! Always keep a growth mindset– your meditation muscles are growing steadily with practice and time.

If it is difficult to sit still, there is no need to be too hard on yourself; it may feel frustrating at first, but you can improve with time and consistency. It's a pillar habit that can positively affect other habits in your life. Most of our habits are misplaced coping skills we built to keep our brains stimulated and invigorated. We might become adrenaline junkies, chasing excitement in high-risk activities, in dating, in our relationships with food or substances, or how we wait for that last-minute pressure rush before a deadline.

.   .   .

While stressful, many of these bad habits we adopted as ways to stimulate our brains, and it can even be addicting. We might get used to drama, high emotions, or ups and downs; if they aren't present, we can feel bored, depressed, unmotivated, or empty. Of course, this happens unconsciously, as we make connections and associations between external stimuli and patterns in how we feel over time. This is also where ADHD can spill into mood disorders. One way to counteract attachment to these coping mechanisms is by doing the opposite of our instincts: run, go, or move — stop, still, and breathe.

Meditation offers a time to get used to slowing down, and disconnecting from our high-energy stress hormones and excitatory neurotransmitters. It lets the body and the brain rest so we can better handle life with more deliberation. Slowing down and grounding my energy is the most rewarding aspects of meditation for my ADHD brain.

You're probably wondering, "Okay, so where do I start? How do I meditate?" Firstly, there's no need for a guru, a class, or major lifestyle changes. All you need is you and your body.

Here's a step-by-step guide to meditation that anyone can follow anytime [4]

1. Sit in a relaxing, comfortable place.
2. Close your eyes, release all muscle tension, and breathe in and out until you have relaxed. You can breath in and exhale for a count of 6 - pausing briefly.

3. Don't force yourself to stop thinking. Rather let your thoughts roam around until they fizzle out. Observe them with open-mindedness. When you notice them, simply go back to focusing on your breathing.

That's it! Meditation, at its core, is that simple, although many variations exist. All it takes is practicing control over your breath and centering yourself anytime your mind escapes from your grip. Over time, you will notice that you can manage your mind much better and can get to a place of peace where almost no thoughts distract you. There is a universal energy that can be felt when you get better at mediation and it is an awe inspiring feeling for me!

Meditation and deep breathing have made a huge impact on calming my daily experience. The exchange of source energy and a calm state is a key part of my mental health. I feel like a squirrel when it comes to sitting down and meditating. Therefore, I don't always practice seated meditation, but I have learned to meditate while I hike, shower, wash dishes or perform any activity that does not require thinking. It's the slow intense exchange of energy is what counts. It is often preceded by or followed by an intention and gratitude for my life.

NATURE BENEFITS ON OUR HEALTH–JAPANESE SHINRIN-YOKU

Nature has its way of effortlessly healing us. Humans were not meant to spend large periods of time indoors, but it's the norm in our modern era. According to the Environmental Protection Agency, Americans tend to spend more than 90% of their time inside. The immense research shows nature's benefits for the body and brain.[5]

Going into nature, surrounded by vibrant greenery and shielded by the thick foliage of trees, provides many advantages for your immunity and stress levels. Micro Compounds called phytoncides from the ground undergo plants' cellular respiration process to find themselves floating in the air we breathe.

Incredibly these phytoncides are antimicrobial and, when breathed in, can strengthen your immune system, lower blood pressure, and alleviate depressive symptoms. Additionally, the ambiance and peace that comes with being in nature reduces mental health issues like anxiety, and focus and improves overall physical well-being since it accompanies breathing fresh air and moving the body.

Spending time in nature can improve your eyesight, increase your vitamin D levels (significant for depression), and promote healthier gut flora; the last two are connected to your mental health.

PLAN MORE GREEN TIME

Expand your mind to the possible activities available for you to do in nature. Just taking a walk or jogging outside in your nearby park can do wonders for your mental health and ADHD. Make sure you find a place that's more green than not, like near the woods or in a grass-field landscape. If you want to spice things up, try activities like doing art outside (or taking outside art classes), doing yoga or tai-chi, boot-camp workouts in the park, and Nordic walking, which is a type of walking that engages the entire body with the help of ski poles. Look online for any outdoor fitness classes available near you. Alternatively, you can keep things simple and take a book with you outside to read on your front porch or backyard.

Family activities include walking together at a county or state park, many offer opportunities to go on a guided walk with a nature expert. Other activities at your disposal are hiking, enjoying a day at the beach, or involving your kids in a team sport like soccer. Try a picnic, or teach your kids how to garden in your backyard. Connect nature with learning for children by going on plant identification expeditions, bug hunting, or collecting pressed flowers. Additionally, the micro- biomes in soil are also great for our gut health.

JAPANESE FOREST BATHING

Immersing yourself in nature has its roots in practically every civilization and culture worldwide, but the Japanese have a name for the experience: Shinrin-Yoku, or forest bathing.Japanese doctors prescribe forest bathing to combat stress in patients.[6]

Shinrin-Yoku is a healing practice, both physically and spiritually, because spending time out in nature almost feels like you are cleansing yourself with it. In other words, you are absorbing it through all of your senses: seeing the colors and details with your eyes; feeling the fresh air and plant-sourced molecules on your skin; breathing it all in, and hearing the sounds of birds chirping, leaves rustling and branches cracking beneath your feet. The experience really is like bathing in a forest.

Remember that Shinrin-yoku is more than just taking a walk in the forest or a park. In reality, it's a meditative experience, a practice in concentrated awareness. It's crucial to lose all thoughts of an objective in this act of forest-bathing to achieve a goal or a motive. Instead, the best way to practice Shinrin-Yoku is to walk without expectation or motive– and let nature take your complete attention.

That may mean leaving behind your phone and any responsibilities wandering around your mind and letting yourself be guided by nature, focusing outside your- self. To better connect with the earth, walk on grass or soil barefoot or lay down in the grass and let yourself get sucked into the peaceful atmosphere. Finding a favorite quiet and beautiful spot to return to is a good idea.

WHY FOREST BATHING PROVIDES ADHD RELIEF

When you, a person with ADHD, spend time in nature, you increase your ability to pay attention to things. According to University of Michigan researchers, there are two types of atten-tion states–directed attention and natural fascination.

.   .   .

The first is a controlled form of attention in which we are focused on a task; it's something that requires us to exercise effort.[7] If we do too much direct focus, it can lead to overuse and fatigue because it is not automatic; it requires a huge behavioral effort; getting too tired from forcing yourself to concentrate leads to impulsivity and distractibility later on.

The second form of attention, fascination, is more automatic and innate, and it often includes a natural inner interest, passion, or attraction to the source of attention. When you are in nature, you cannot help but switch to fascination. Who isn't drawn in by the magnetic and peaceful nature of earth's beauty? *Fascination* is a relaxed form of focus that is more rejuvenating than taxing. It boosts your energy and reduces impulsivity, allowing you to feel more inspired, more creative, and ready for longer periods of concentration. An extra benefit is that it improves short-term memory.

We can all attest to the good feelings we get from spending an entire day in nature. The next time you find yourself in nature, take five minutes to do a nature bath, using all your senses and feel the call that only nature can provide. To go even deeper into self-care, let's explore different ways to promote and improve mental health in the next chapter.

∽

"Meditation is choosing not to engage in the drama of the mind but, elevating the mind to its highest potential." –
Amit Ray

Chapter 8

Hypnosis, Visualization & Affirmations

I constantly struggled to figure out what would work for my ADHD brain, so I read and listened to loads of self-help books. I have learned that our beliefs impact our lives in profound ways. A good friend of mine always told her kids, "You don't always get a choice in life, but you do get to choose your thoughts and how you feel." Positive or negative, your beliefs affect your feelings, which in turn affect your body and, very possibly, the outcome of your life.

Concerning your spirit, you may find it difficult to see the practical techniques you can use to improve its state. We've got meditation, breathing, and nature — all habits you can easily implement in your life. However, there is an expansive world of opportunity for elevating your spirit's well-being through methods like hypnosis, visualization, and affirmation.

Because ADHD is a brain-based disorder does not mean it is out of our hands. We *can* take charge of our minds and will, just as anyone else. As Jose Silva once said, "The greatest discovery you'll ever make is the potential of your own mind." We follow in his footsteps in an attempt to release the full potential of our minds and spirit with simple yet powerful exercises.

Before we do that, let's discuss a key measurement or marker of progress for your spirit's well-being: Self-love.

WHY SELF-LOVE MATTERS

Taking care of your spirit is nothing without self-love. Self-love is when you treat yourself as you would someone you love unconditionally.

Self-love, some say, is the foundation for the love you give. When we feel healthy and whole within ourselves, being there for others as a stable source of love is much easier, less energy-draining, more fulfilling, and more genuine. It's like trying to share a half-full cup with others instead of sharing a full cup; there's more of you to go around.

First of all, what is self-love? Rather than a sense of narcissism and selfishness, self-love is about feeling accomplished and proud of yourself when you do something wonderful. If you were to analyze your interactions with yourself, you'd find that even when you achieve a task or something positive occurs, you might be in the habit of brushing it off. I understand. Society has wired many of us to be "humble" by downplaying positive things. In adulthood, this translates to telling ourselves that our accomplishments weren't that great, that we could have done better, or that others have been able to do more.

Practicing self-love forces us to do the opposite. It allows us to open our eyes to the positive things in life and in us, to be grateful and more willing to treat ourselves with respect. Prioritize caring for yourself, not always giving more to the people around you and brushing off your own needs and desires, and boundaries; giving yourself breaks; putting yourself first; and focusing on your health just as much as others, if not more.

Self-love isn't selfish. It's simple self-preservation. With it, you can take better care of your diet, fitness, and sleep more than you take care of responsibilities, work, and favors. Selflessness is only valuable if it isn't at the expense of yourself. Moreover, self-care means caring for yourself beyond basic necessities like showering, eating, and sleeping. It also means taking time to recover or do things that make you happy. It's also how you treat yourself in your internal conversations. When you have self-love, you are proud of yourself, like yourself, enjoy spending time with yourself, appreciate yourself, and have faith in your abilities and actions. Give yourself permission to put yourself first. There's nothing wrong with it, no need to feel guilty. Additionally, do not settle for less by turning down the opportunities others want to give to you.

Practicing self-love can seem so vague and abstract that it can be hard to practice. How do you love yourself? Does it involve constantly thinking of yourself above others? How do you feel about it authentically? The idea may be hard to wrap your head, but a self-care routine does have several options for self-love-directed moves. Including it in your routine consistently can improve your overall self-image and increase your feelings of well-being and peace within your spirit.

A self-care routine is a preventative measure against burnout, fatigue, anxiety, and mental distress. And it requires mental discipline to handle and carry out daily. You also learn more about yourself and your limits, emotionally, mentally, and physically. You can connect better with your spirit and understand your individual needs regarding ADHD, observing yourself better so you can know how to address your needs in the best way to live your life and thrive.

With greater self-esteem, more confidence, and less anxiety, you get to unlock more personal growth because you are giving yourself the care you need. If you're always in go-go-go mode, you won't be able to self-reflect or experience self-development. Genuinely loving yourself increases your awareness of your behaviors and inner self, so you can avoid being a people pleaser or living out of a trauma response Some of the most recommended ways to boost self-love are affirmations, journaling, and practicing mindful eating.

DAILY AFFIRMATIONS

A technique that can take less than five minutes of your day is reciting affirmations that promote self-love. Affirmations are just statements affirming what you want to instill into your belief system. In this case, you want to affirm. Some may brush off affirmations as something that does not work or as a form of lying to yourself. Others might call it toxic positivity since, in some people's hands, affirmations can be used as a way to ignore some characteristics or facts that they may actually need to face. However, for improving your self-esteem and boosting your spirit in the face of ADHD, affirmations offer a way to fight any negative thoughts.

If you have a negative self-image and lie to yourself, the more likely you are to believe it, and your current negative beliefs about yourself might not be completely accurate anyway (i.e., "I can't do anything right!", "Why am I such a failure?") and other thoughts that reveal low self-worth.

The way you choose your thoughts matters. Affirmations are basically the process of reprogramming your mind with new thoughts that you intentionally make for a new belief system that makes you feel confident, happy, content, resilient, and so on. Repeating affirmations fight an inner dialogue or mental chatter that does not benefit you. It brings more positivity to your life by having more useful, optimistic thoughts; when used consistently, this does work because it increases your belief in these new thoughts, building the mindset you want.

Over time even if it feels like it's not working right now, it will be instilled in you as you repeat your favorite affirmations every day. Don't let others criticize that you are like Stuart Smalley from Saturday Night Live. It works!
For example, some ideas for affirmations include:

1. I appreciate and love myself.
2. I am working hard to improve every day.

3. I am worthy as I am.
4. I am capable of achieving what I want to achieve.
5. The more I practice, the easier it gets.
6. I respect myself and my boundaries.
7. It doesn't have to be perfect; it just has to be done.
8. Failure is better than not trying.
9. I believe in myself.

One of the best habits is doing your affirmations in bed every morning or night or picking a few key ones and saying them daily; it may feel weird at first, but you will feel an instant mood shift.

Another hack to try is Mel Robbin's 'High Five Habit', ("The High Five Habit, Hayhouse Publisher, September, 2021). She advocates giving yourself a physical high five in a mirror several times a day. It really is amazing how you feel when you acknowledge yourself like you would a good friend!

JOURNALING

When you have ADHD, you might struggle with long-term memory issues on top of your working memory issues. I've found journaling to fill in the missing piece in my memory and in my mental judgment. There are immense therapeutic benefits of having a journal into which you can brain-dump all your worries and ideas.

. . .

When you look back on your older journal entries, you can understand yourself better, see progress, reflect on your behavior and emotions and use that information to improve your life now. It offers you an outlet to vent in a healthier way. Or it can provide a space for you to further solidify your goals, values, positive beliefs, and self-love affirmations. The most important thing journaling provides is an intimate knowledge of who you are, which allows you to respect yourself more naturally.

PRACTICE MINDFUL EATING

The saying goes, "The way to a man's heart is through his stomach." Turns out, this applies to pretty much anybody. In this case, it's important to rethink how you eat just as much as you enrich your diet. Mindful eating is a recommendation that applies to anyone, not just those with ADHD.

Eating mindfully is when you take your meals with more deliberation and purpose. In this fast-paced world, we've grown accustomed to eating fast. Our breakfasts are skipped or gobbled down in the car; our snacks are eaten mindlessly as we focus on other tasks, pick up a banana on our way out or use the fastfood drive-thru on our way home from work. The opposite of this is to slow down, respect our meal times, and choose, make, and eat our food with purpose and presence.

How does mindful eating promote self-love and a healthy spirit? As I mentioned before, food quality has a significant impact on ADHD brains, and at the same time, ADHD increases our risk of using food in unhealthy ways, like overeating and consuming too much sugar. Mindful eating addresses this by allowing us to be more conscious of what and how we eat. In that way, we also become more satisfied and fulfilled.

It's simple: To eat mindfully, you must make an effort to focus on your food and savor it. What helps is to pretend you are eating for the first time or that you are a judge on a cooking show trying out a dish for an audience. You must take small bites, eat and chew slowly, and think about the taste, flavor, texture, and smell. Be aware of how your body feels while you eat to become more connected with your hunger and satiety cues.

HYPNOTHERAPY & ADHD

Hynotherapy sounds like treatment from a 20th-century asylum, but it's not that far-fetched. While the research is limited, it's growing to support evidence for hypnotherapy.

Studies reveal significant effects of hypnotherapy on improving a person's behavioral issues, including characteristics of ADHD. For instance, it has been found to help improve self-esteem, decrease stress, increase self-efficacy (which is your belief in yourself and your abilities), and even your overall sense of control over your life.

Even if most of the effect of hypnotherapy is placebo, it's still an effective option for reprogramming your mind. After all, it uses the same principles as meditation and incorporates aspects of the Silva Method. What is important to know is that hypnotherapy, even if done by a certified hypnotherapist, cannot be done without your consent. In other words, all hypnosis is self-hypnosis. That means that, whether you decide to see a hypnotherapy professional or not, you can perform self-hypnosis at any time in the comfort of your own home.

Doing hypnosis is easy — it's a lot like meditation:

1. First, get comfortable and sit in a peaceful place.
2. Have a goal in mind, a long-term goal preferably that you can work on consistently for several weeks.
3. Try to stick to one goal for a period of time.
4. Focus your line of sight on something in front of you.
5. You don't necessarily need to close your eyes, but if you help you avoid distractions, then do so.
6. Get into the deep breathing groove until you are relaxed, physically and mentally.
7. If it helps, visualize yourself in your desired place, which increases your sense of calm. For instance, imagine a beachside hammock or a beautiful grassland surrounded by flowers and mountains.
8. Self-hypnosis can rely a bit more on affirmations. Pretend you are a hypnotist in your mind, telling yourself affirmations that guide you. For instance, start by affirming that you are relaxed and getting more and more relaxed every second.
9. When you feel you've sunk deeper into "hypnosis," turn your attention to the goal, you set. Now, either visualize that goal in a vibrant holographic way, even feeling your emotions of living the goal, then repeat a set of related affirmations in your mind until you feel them sink into your consciousness.

10. When you feel ready to finish, go back to your breathing for a few minutes. Slowly wiggle your toes and fingers, limbs, and other body parts until you return to the present. Or you can do a backward countdown until you snap your eyes open.

The benefits of self-hypnosis show up after a few weeks of consistent effort, and reported benefits include; deep relaxation, assisting with insomnia, pain control, and increased intuition. With time and repetition, the brain gets used to new neural patterns and allows those changes you make during each session to appear in your daily life. These meditations help to lay down new positive neuro-pathways in your mind for an overall positive outlook in your waking state.

All of the above methods contribute to an honorable aim of achieving mindfulness in everyday life. Taking time for yourself and giving yourself the care you need will go a long way to helping you to be aware of your feelings and state of mind. As such, they are a way to work on ADHD symptoms and upgrade your life. Let's sink even deeper into that goal with more mindful training in Chapter 10.

~

"If you can dream it, you can do it." – Walt Disney

Chapter 9

Mindfulness Training

M indfulness, while the finale of the spiritual aspect of managing ADHD, is a critical component of well-being. So far, we've only touched on it, but understanding it thoroughly is key to unlocking mental and emotional well-being.

As neuroscientist Sam Harris said, "How we pay attention to the present moment largely determines the character of our experience, and therefore, the quality of our lives." That's what mindfulness with ADHD is all about. We round off the book with tips on mindfulness bound to determine your self-care."

WHAT IS MINDFULNESS?

If ADHD is scattered attention, being impulsive and reactive, becoming overwhelmed by everything going on in life, and forgetting or failing to slow down to reflect on your behaviors to better control them next time, then mindfulness is the exact opposite.

To be mindful is to be completely aware of the ***present moment*** and all of its facts: time, place, sensation, being, feeling, and everything that makes up *consciousness*. When you practice mindfulness, you are totally present with the activity unfolding around and the energy within you. We learn what you are currently doing in the now, what thoughts your mind is generating, and what are your senses are taking in? If you tune into all of it and experience it truly, we are deeply appreciative of what we have and our very existence. It's a profound experience when you are able to be fully present and *conscious*.

What does that mean? You might wonder, "Don't I already experience that stuff anyway?" Yes, but often we don't take the time to stop and really explore that experience with mental presence. When we go through any experience, our mind can be miles away from the present moment, either trying to escape the sensations or trying to judge the situation, or formulating a solution to counteract the displeasing feelings. It is that lack of mindfulness that leads to reactivity; we make a move without conscious thought. Those reactions operate from an unconscious drive that was conditioned in us from youth. When overwhelmed, we jump to these conditioned reactions, which evolution has allowed us to access automatically to save time. Unfortunately, they don't always help us. And when we have ADHD, those conditioned impulses can be even more uninformed and risky.

. . .

Mindfulness creates a space between the current experience we are feeling and our potential reaction. In other words, training ourselves to be present at the moment helps give us time and awareness to make an informed *response*. Responding, rather than reacting, gives us control and power over our behaviors.

When we aren't necessarily going through a high-emotion situation, when we are just resting and decide to tap into being mindful, we get another benefit – self-reflection. We can observe where we are in that moment, following the preceding events of the day or the week, and take inventory of how we feel, what thoughts we have, and how those events accumulated into who we are now. Mindfulness allows us to access insight into our experience and ourselves. The caveat is that we must approach this awareness with gentle compassion towards ourselves, rather than being judgmental and beating ourselves up for any mistakes we make. Mindfulness requires a nonjudgmental attitude, and while its main purpose for ADHD is to rev up those attention and self-regulatory muscles, it's also to get to know your spirit better.

Mindfulness allows us to reflect and later choose our response rather than act on conditioned impulses:

1. Put time into your scheduled routine to be mindful, whether you choose to meditate or not.
2. Observe. Simply be in the present moment. Don't try to do anything. Pay attention to the moment as you live in it, without any judgment or purpose.
3. If you do have any thoughts, let them pass. Pretend they are not you. What you are is the space around your thought, the higher consciousness surrounding the little wheedling thoughts that nudge your

attention. Let them pass by like clouds or a fly buzzing around you.

4. If your mind wanders, don't stress. You're still doing it right. Get used to the act of getting back to the present. With practice, this snapping out of the mind-wandering/daydreaming state will be easier, and you will be better able to catch yourself in times of inattention.

5. First, use what you learned from deep breathing to get into a relaxed state. Breathing will be your main point of attention, as it keeps you grounded in the present moment. Make sure you are comfortable in a quiet place.

6. Bring attention to your body. Start with your source of air, i.e., your chest/diaphragm, as you feel the air go into you and out of you.

7. Let your awareness travel throughout your entire body, feeling what your legs are doing, making sure the bottoms are flat and grounded on the floor, and then notice that your arms are relaxed and rested naturally. Make sure your muscles are not tense. Straighten your posture gently without feeling uncomfortable or tight. Let your head be positioned naturally.

8. You can close your eyes or keep them centered on a single point level with your line of sight.

9. When you face challenges from your mind, just remember one thing: BE. There is nothing complex about mindfulness; it's really just about *being*, not doing, thinking, wondering, doubting, or judging; it's about being and letting yourself BE. Just BEING is deeply underrated. It helps you to be present in the moment you are in, allowing you to enjoy life more fully.

MINDFULNESS & ADHD

Here's how mindfulness works to alleviate ADHD symptoms and, with regular long-term practice, manage them permanently. Mindfulness forces you to get used to being aware of your daily thoughts and emotional state; with that awareness, you can better choose your response.

Think about it – thoughts and feelings occur instantly, without awareness, and that split-second can drive us to act on our first-line impulses. In other words, we react without considering the consequences of having an actual choice in the matter.

Mindfulness physically changes your brain. It improves the prefrontal cortex, the part of the brain in charge of attentional abilities and self-regulation. If weak or not exercised properly, this prefrontal cortex is involved in poor executive functioning, thus leading to reduced planning skills and problems with managing your impulses.

According to research at UCLA, when people with ADHD practiced mindfulness for two and a half hours a week, along with a short meditation session daily, reduced symptoms of depression, anxiety, inattention, and scattered focus. As a bonus, it also increases dopamine levels which our brains are always grateful to have.[1]

Chapter 9

MAINTAINING MINDFULNESS

Say you have gotten good at achieving a mindful state during your meditation settings. Now how can you maintain mindfulness throughout the day? You can step back into a state of simply feeling, sensing, and experiencing the present without any critical thoughts that take you far into the air. This is possible by focusing on three main actions in any given moment: switching your attention to your current experience, accepting it and yourself, and simply feeling yourself breathing, deep or not. Doing these three things can make you mindful within a minute.

- Focus your attention: If you forget to be mindful throughout the day, it helps to keep a post-it note around you at all times to remind yourself. Then, focus on your surroundings and your senses, taking it all in. An exercise I like to do mentally is to point out one thing I am doing.
- Accept yourself: Do not be judgmental toward yourself; accept yourself as you are in the moment. For instance, say you have been working on an important assignment with a close deadline, and you're frustrated and stressed and unable to concentrate on it long enough to make real progress. Stop and focus your attention externally. Bring your attention down to your body rather than your head, and feel the sensations. The energy you feel can take on a very spiritual feeling that washes over your head and body.
- Focus on your breathing: Finally, the one we always come back to...always take deep breaths as you do this to further find an anchor for your attention.

Breathing and focusing on your breathing helps you better pay attention to how your body feels and senses at that moment.

This three-step process is just a quick way to quickly switch to a state of mindfulness. However, I will introduce to you now a few specific mindfulness exercises you can try to figure out what works for you best.

MINDFULNESS EXERCISES

Try these unique mindfulness exercises if you struggle with bringing attention to something specific in your experience.

BODY SCAN MEDITATION

This meditation allows you to reconnect with your body. Lie on your back, extend your legs, keep your arms at your sides, palms up, and focus attention on each part of your body from toe to head and vice versa.

If this doesn't change your relationship with your body, it will change your relationship with discomfort; you can stay more tuned in even if you don't like what you're feeling because the reason why we unconsciously disconnect from awareness of our bodies and minds is that it makes us uncomfortable to feel those feelings in the first place; when you can get to a place where you can feel them without issue, you're good. You become more experienced in feeling uncomfortable or dissatisfied feelings and still being okay. Over time, you will be able to stay still and feel all sensations, both in your body and emotionally, and be present before learning to allow the sensation to fade as you return to the present.

A body scan helps you be better at staying in the current experience, even if you feel overwhelmed physically and emotionally. It reduces the chaotic feelings because most of our negative feelings come from not knowing why and what it is we are feeling. We try to distract ourselves from it, which keeps it stuck in our body and manifests in other ways, like impulsive behavior, interpersonal problems, or maladaptive habits.

It can bring your full attention to real-time experiences happening in the present moment; be with bad sensations and notice what happens without judging or trying to fix it.

Start by doing a 30-40 minute body scan every week, with a 5-minute body scan daily, depending on how much time you have to spare. You can do it in bed, either while waking or just before falling asleep.

First, close your eyes. Breathe in and out and notice your body's contact with other things like your chair, the floor, or even the clothes against your skin. After you get into the groove of things, begin deep breathing and start the body scan either from the crown of your head down or your toes up; slowly scan your limbs and body parts one by one. Look out for a body like tingling, tightness, heat, coolness, buzzing, pulsing, itching, numbing, nausea, etc. if you feel vaguely uncomfortable, sit with that. If you feel neutral, take note of that too. No matter what, do not judge.

SITTING MEDITATION

Sit either on a chair with feet against the floor or on the floor cross-legged; keep your back straight and neutral; there's no need to bend over backward to keep its board straight. Now focus on your deep breathing. How you sit matters because if you are uncomfortable, you won't be able to concentrate. You don't want to be readjusting all the time. If you sit in a chair, it can be easy to maintain a straight back and good posture, so long as your knees are at a 90-degree angle. Your head and neck should be aligned with your spine.

Another position you can do is to kneel, which allows you to keep a straight back comfortable. Ensure a cushion beneath your knees or between your rear and heels.

WALKING MEDITATION

Doing a walking meditation may be the best option for people with ADHD, as it keeps them stimulated and engaged while they tap into mindfulness. When doing this, ensure you are in a place with little foot traffic and distraction or dangerous risks, like a big park or grassy area. Talk a walk, but go slowly, taking your time and really concentrating your focus on every step and movement.

MINDFUL TRAINING

Research shows that both poor attention and executive functioning deficits are common traits of people with ADHD. Therefore any treatments that can strengthen those processes are helpful. Many studies have measured the impact of mindfulness training in experienced meditators (Taylor et al., 2013), and find that even brief training with meditation novices yields improvements in attention and can be a powerful alternative treatment for people with ADHD.[2]

While all this breathing and mindful training are crucial to grounding your mind/spirit with ADHD, it's time to express your spirit. With that said, let's move on to the undeniable connection between creativity and ADHD and how you can maximize it to the best of your ability in the next chapter.

∾

"You are the sky.
Everything else is just the weather."
– Pema Chodron

Chapter 10

Creativity: The Ultimate Advantage of ADHD

So far, we've talked about managing the not-so-helpful parts of ADHD, like the inattention and lack of focus, scattered thoughts and forgetting important things, and the inability to control one's impulses.

What about the positive, the unlocked superpowers that we will be able to access upon harnessing ADHD? Now, it's time to uncover one of the most powerful gifts that ADHD provides: creativity, an element that is more vital than you might think, especially for your health, well-being, and success in life.

Creativity certainly is the ultimate superpower of ADHD. Through creativity, the ADHD mind is free to expand, think divergently, and come up with unique new possibilities. ADHD folks really shine in the world of creativity!

Chapter 10

ADHD AND CREATIVITY

Some of the "negative" parts of ADHD that don't fit in with the modern, fast-paced world can actually propel us to perform better in other contexts. For instance, the ability to jump from one topic to another mentally and take impulsive action can fuel our creativity. Neil Hallowell put it perfectly when he said: "What is creativity after all, but impulsivity gone right?"

Creativity is when we funnel the chaos of ADHD into a concentrated stream of energy to generate something beautiful, inspirational, and innovative. Making more effort to express our creativity can help us manage our other more destructive ADHD symptoms.

Long ago, I assumed that because I was too creative, too free-flowing, and passionate, I needed to force myself into the mold that made people in the modern age more productive. ADHD lives are at odds with real-world efficiency and production. We try our best, but real-world robotic work regimes counter our nature. ADHD brains prefer freedom, exploration, and possibility!

By repressing those innate drives, we limit ourselves in both logical and non-linear ways of thinking. Not using our creative ability hampers our daily motivation and efficiency, and dulls our spirit since we are not using the amazing well of creative energy within. If we choose to access that well regularly, we can nourish both sides – the part of us that must at times conform and the part of us that must be let free. On the one hand, we can be impulsive, chaotic, sensitive, and playful, which may not work in conventional work settings. On the other hand, these same features allow us to develop novel, useful solutions to ordinary tasks. Our ability to think outside of the box, have a wider lens on the world, solve problems, take risks, and hyperfocus when interested all contribute to our successful creative pursuits.

WHAT MAKES PEOPLE WITH ADHD CREATIVE

What systems make the ADHD brain more likely to assess creativity? Ironically, the features of ADHD that are unwelcome in conventional work environments are the same ones that fuel creativity.

Take a distractible mind; for example, such a mind cannot focus for long periods on tedious activities. Trying to do a simple task can be hard because our brains can't help but bounce from one random topic to another without any particular connection between them (as far as other people can see). In reality, this distractibility is lending a hand to our *divergent thinking skills.*

Divergent thinking is the ability to start from a single idea and branch off into multiple different ideas or perspectives that are not immediately obvious to others.[1] We store in our brains a lot of stuff that isn't accessible to us until something triggers a series of connections between a bunch of seemingly unrelated ideas. This allows us to see things in myriad ways, thus allowing us to be creative in forming completely new ideas or inventions. As opposed to convergent thinking, which is a narrowed, focused form of problem-solving that relies on logic and proven methods.

. . .

Another brain system involved in ADHD is the ability to overcome worldly limitations when using creativity. Research has found that knowledge or existing information about a concept can actually deter people from imagining completely new things.[2]

For instance, a product development team, may ask someone to invent a new animal, recipe, or food. This can be difficult since most people base their creations on previous versions of those things. Expanding your definition of a concept is challenging because of what you already know about it. While you can be creative about it and innovate something, it won't be as unique or original as it could be. Alternately, people with ADHD actually have some immunity to this limitation. Studies have shown that they can go beyond the limited characteristics of an already existing thing and offer completely new artistic interpretations of it.

Additionally, when approaching a task or topic we are passionate about, then it's game over. Anything we find interesting can propel us into hyperfocus mode, making us nearly unstoppable in a task we enjoy, pouring all our attention and creative energy into doing our best in it.

UNLOCK YOUR ADHD GENIUS

Albert Einstein once said, "Everybody is a genius. But if you judge a fish by its ability to climb a tree, it will live its whole life believing that it is stupid." When you use your creativity properly, you can be a genius too. Creativity has been given a backseat in our educational system for far too long. The current educational structure is not suited to the ADHD brain, and as many of us are losing the capacity for prolonged focused attention, future institutional change may be inevitable.

It's no coincidence that so many of the world's artistic talents either were confirmed with ADHD or thought to have signs of ADHD. Da Vinci, Van Gogh, and Picasso all displayed classic traits of ADHD hyperfocus. Additionally, each artist's massive diversity of work gives us insight into their divergent thinking patterns. Even if it is a coincidence, it's clear that there is a link between ADHD brains and the potential for creativity, if only we could just use it to the best of our ability.

Are all ADHD brains artistic geniuses? Probably not, but artistic pursuits are a great way to harness our pent-up energies for positive outcomes.

With the right tools and context, you can unlock your genius. The distractibility that prevents people with ADHD from doing well in focused contexts allows them to thrive regarding creativity and original ideas. This is perfect for innovative fields like art, writing, engineering, cooking, decorating, building, creating, making music, and working with computers. It even shows up in daydreaming (which isn't always maladaptive), imagining our goals and futures, planning a trip, or managing an event. How about our fidgety nature? Creative pursuits are the perfect outlet for working with our hands. People are meant to create, and even more so if you have ADHD. As you can see, this creativity, when we tap into it, offers us extremely valuable skills that are necessary for many careers. Don't let it go to waste just because it goes against the grain.

THE DOWNSIDE OF NOT USING YOUR CREATIVITY

Untapped creativity can be negative. It can lead to a sense of lack, aimlessness, and resentment. In fact, you can go so far as to say that not using your creativity or expressing yourself can be bad for your health.

Everyone needs a way to express themselves; that is an inherent truth of being human. When it comes to adults with ADHD, we have probably spent a long time masking and pretending to be someone we are not. Perhaps for you, that means forcing yourself to lean more toward your logical left brain. Maybe you had to be more strict with yourself to concentrate on a project or work that didn't resonate with you. Doing this without leaning on your creative right brain can lead to burnout. Not only does it oppose who we are, but it can also drain our energy.

In fact, not tapping into our creativity can wreak havoc on productivity and motivation. If ignored, it can be harmful. If you think of creativity as energy within you, not using it can be bad because it essentially rots within you with nowhere to go. Overall, it can lead to misery, irritability, and bad health. Quite literally, it affects your body and mind. If you have some random or mysterious physical or emotional ailments, you may need to embrace your creativity to heal. Art as therapy has long been proven valuable in helping trauma patients recover.

Creativity in harmony with who we are, not what others want us to be, is the key. It is literally who we are, manifested in physical forms outside ourselves. Accepting that and making a deliberate decision to engage with your creativity can lead to higher self-esteem, better life satisfaction, and more energy and patience to drive through the necessary tasks you don't want to do.

POSITIVE OUTCOMES OF CREATIVITY

Utilizing our creativity can lead to many advantages. Being creative increases our sense of purpose, satisfaction, joy, well-being, self-esteem, confidence, productivity, and sense of accomplishment. All humans are meant to create, and this truth is even more so for the ADHD person.

Creative endeavors foster self-actualization and joy in our lives. Self-actualization is the point at which we level up and match up to our hidden potential. When we live in survival mode, which many people with ADHD are doing, we are barely functioning, only making it through by the seat of our pants and trying to keep up with the stressful, dissatisfying parts of work and life. In this mode, we are not self-actualized.

. . .

The importance of holistic management of ADHD is the main message I want to drive home. This is because this solution addresses the facets of life that you can tackle to get *out* of survival mode. When you have covered your food, sleep, exercise, health, and mental health, you are in a place where you have more value to add to the world. Your cup is fuller, life is inspired, and you are ready to express yourself to the universe.

In simpler words, creativity helps us understand who we are. At the same time, we can let out the inner emotional and spiritual energy that would otherwise manifest as restlessness and hyperactivity. We can channel impulsivity in healthy ways, like in artistic pursuits.

HOW TO ADD MORE CREATIVITY TO YOUR LIFE

We are meant to be creative, whatever your desired outlet. Above all, be who you are and do what you love. Embrace your unique creativity. We must carve out time daily, for creativity, just like exercise. Embrace creativity as a tool to harness your ultimate superpower!

GET TO THE STARTING LINE

Just start. Maybe you used to have a creative pursuit when you were younger that you left behind when you entered the real adult world. Or maybe you have never been into anything "artistic." That's the thing. Creativity isn't just about art. It's about *creation*, generating, and constructing. You can apply creativity to just about anything in life and make a funky time out of normal tasks.

Start with creating a beautiful meal. Try my favorite, the Buddha Bowl rainbow salad, using as many colors in the rainbow as you have on hand. Start with a cup of cooked red rice as the base. Dice colorful vegetables finely and add a triangle of color around the bowl, like hours on a clock. Top with a peanut or cashew cream recipe you can find on the internet. Not only will you have a beautiful creative dinner, it will also fuel your body and mind. For many years, cooking was my only creative outlet when I had limited time. My family believes that creating beautiful salads and amazing soups is one of my superpowers.

MAKE TIME FOR CREATIVITY

Don't wait until you have a spark of inspiration or until you're done with your work. Add time for creativity into your routine, perhaps during your breaks or somewhere early in your evening routine before bed if you are a night owl. Whatever it may be, add it to your routine.

If you don't have any creative hobbies, it is time to try something new. That may mean buying some paint, clay, and craft materials. Try knitting, sewing, or volunteering to teach art in your kid's class. Sharing your talent gives you a sense of pride and accomplishment as well. When I did this, and loved teaching art. I felt an immense boost in my confidence and mental health. Letting out your creativity is a form of self-care; it makes you feel better in every way, and you're creating cool stuff in the process. Creative endeavors are important to prioritize in your life.

CREATE ANYTHING

If you want to take time in your day to actually, formally create something artistic, explore your options; with so many possibilities out there, you'll never get bored. A painting, sculpture, garden, healthy meal, whatever it is you love. It is all about the journey and the process, not the end result. Once you succeed in smaller projects, move on to taking up a visual art or an instrument.

If this is something you've never tried before: yes, you may fail in the beginning. However, you must embrace where you are and give yourself the break; you're a beginner! Don't let perfection stop you; nobody can draw a figure on the first go around. With consistent practice, you can monitor your own success through video (musical instrument), a progressive portfolio, or journaling. With consistency, watch yourself and your creativity blossom over time!

Find a creative outlet that lights your fire, make practicing it a new habit, create a daily routine and see what creative superpower you are capable of. I am constantly amazed at what creativity come out of children with ADHD, so as ADHD adults, we have cute little role-models!

Conclusion

Accepting and managing your ADHD holistically is a long-term, sustainable solution to maximizing your potential. Although ADHD is a hereditary neurological disorder, you can and must embrace it to manage it properly. By focusing on the three important components of wellness: body, mind, and spirit, you can help holistically manage your ADHD, opening up your own unique gifts and power!

As we learned, managing the body aspect of ADHD, and making lifestyle changes across your diet, sleep, and exercise are vital and foundational. Stave off brain fog and inflammation by filling up on whole foods, vitamins, minerals, and blood-sugar-balancing protein. Stay away from substances that can be addictive or make your symptoms worse. Exercise at least 150 minutes weekly to maintain energy, improve concentration, channel impulsive hyperactivity, and sleep well. It is important the you fight to avoid the underlying sleep issues that are rampant among people with ADHD by improving your sleep schedule and sleep hygiene.

When it comes to the mind, learning to set SMART goals, both short-term and long-term can help us be more deliberate and motivated in our day-to-day lives. When we choose goals that are meaningful to us and break them down into doable steps, we can reduce procrastination, forgetfulness, and lack of productivity. We can help ourselves meet those daily and long-term goals by structuring our day and environment for success.

Finally, do not forget about nurturing our spirit, which consists of improving our mindset, mental health, self-concept, and self-realization. We can do this by making a habit of deep breathing, going out into nature, meditating, self-hypnosis, affirmations for self-love, and visualizing our potential. All of these tips make us more mindful of the present and better able to snap out of our unconscious ADHD behaviors. When we can be more aware of ourselves, we can better express our beautiful spirit through the natural creativity source within anyone with ADHD.

Take care of the mind, body, and spirit triad– these are the building blocks for good health and mental clarity. If you cherish your body, mind, and spirit, you'll be paid back in ways you never dreamed of.

Either positive or negative, health is a choice that you make, and it all comes down to daily decisions and actions. Once you take responsibility for your life and start making positive choices, you will become an ADHD superhero! Having tamed your ADHD, you can make them work in your favor.

When you make healthy and consistent changes, you can experience the positive side of ADHD—boundless energy, newfound hyperfocus, unique productivity, and expanded creativity! There will be no stopping you as you prepare to conquer your universe!

Never feel less-than because it *seems* like you aren't moving forward in life or can do the same things easily as another. The important thing is that most ADHD symptoms can be improved with these healthier practices, whether you are on the mild or extreme end of the spectrum.

All the methods I provided in this book can be used by *anyone* to reduce any struggles relevant to ADHD, diagnosed or not. If you suspect you need medication, it is not recommended to white-knuckle ADHD with these methods alone. Always make sure to check with your doctor first and ask about a combination of approaches. If you have a severe case, it's best to tackle that brain chemistry first before you start drafting a rigid schedule and buying fidget spinners.

It can feel exhausting at times, but managing your day-to-day routine is important. These healthy building blocks are essential in a holistic approach to ADHD symptoms and overall health. Take the first steps today by picking just a few cornerstone life-style changes to implement into your day. To stick to it consistently, keep it as simple as possible! The crucial thing is that you start targeting your ADHD from a holistic mindset for yourself, your family, your goals, your well-being, and your growth.

Conclusion

WE are all beings of light and love; some of us just have more energy, creativity, compassion and humor than others!

Life's blessings to you on your unique and healthy ADHD journey.

∾

*"There is nothing we cannot do,
if we harness the power within us."*

~ Tao Porchon-Lynch

Endnotes

~

Introduction:

1. Hallowell, E. (2021, January 12). Undiagnosed Adult ADHD or ADD: Why Diagnosis Can Save a Life. ADDitude. Retrieved July 7, 2022, from https://www.additudemag.com/undiagnosed-adult-adhd-diagnosis- symptoms/

Chapter 1

1. ADHD Diet Plan: Foods to Eat & Avoid to Help ADD Symptoms. (n.d.). ADDitude. Retrieved August 4, 2022, from https://www.additudemag.com/adhd-diet-nutrition-sugar
2. Omega-3 Benefits to ADHD Brains: Fish Oil for Focus. (2021, May 5). ADDitude. Retrieved August 4, 2022, from https://www.additudemag.- com/adhd-omega-3-benefits

3. Newmark, S. (n.d.). The ADHD Diet Plan: Healthy
   Foods and Supplements for Kids & Adults.
   ADDitude. Retrieved August 4, 2022, from
   https://www.additudemag.com/adhd-diet-for-
   kids-food-fix/

4. Carlson, L. (2017, June 22). Is your brain on fire?
   Symptoms of brain inflammation | ChiroPro
   Performance Center. | ChiroPro Performance Center.
   Retrieved July 1 , 2022, from https://chiroproperfor-
   mance.com/is- your-brain-on-fire-symptoms-of-
   brain-inflammation/

5. Carlson, L. (2017, June 22). Is your brain on fire?
   Symptoms of brain inflammation | ChiroPro
   Performance Center. | ChiroPro Performance Center.
   Retrieved July 1 , 2022, from https://chiroproperfor-
   mance.com/is- your-brain-on-fire-symptoms-of-
   brain-inflammation/

6. Legg, T. J. (2019, September 18). ADHD and
   Alcohol: How They're Linked Plus Interactions &
   Risk Factors. Healthline. Retrieved July 19, 2022,
   from https://www.healthline.com/health/adhd-and-
   alcohol#risk-factors

7. Vath, C. (n.d.). Caffeine and ADHD: Is This Natural
   Treatment Safe & Effective? ADDitude. Retrieved
   August 4, 2022, from https://www.addi-
   tudemag.com/adhd-caffeine-treatment/

8. Pandolfo, P., Machado, N., Köfalvi, A., Takahashi, R.
   N., & Cunha, R. A. (2013). Caffeine regulates
   frontal-corticostriatal dopamine transporter density
   and improves attention and cognitive deficits in an
   animal model of attention deficit hyperactivity
   disorder,. European Neuropsychopharmacology,,
   23(4), 317-328.
   https://doi.org/10.1016/j.euroneuro.2012.04.011.

9. Whole-Foods, Plant-Based Diet: A Detailed Beginner's Guide. (2018, June 12). Healthline. Retrieved August 4, 2022, from https://www.healthline.- com/nutrition/plant-based-diet-guide

10. Easy Vegan Breakfast Hash with Veggies and Beans. (2021, March 12). Karissa's Vegan Kitchen. Retrieved July 18, 2022, from https://www.karis-sasvegankitchen.com/bean-potato-veggie-breakfast-hash/

11. Fawley, C. D. (n.d.). Vegan Curried Chickpea Salad Recipe | MamaSezz Plant Based Prepared Meals. MamaSezz. Retrieved July 27, 2022, from https://www.mamasezz.com/blogs/recipes/curried-chickpea-salad-recipe

12. Fawley, C. D. (n.d.). Creamy Plant-Based Avocado Pasta Recipe | MamaSezz Plant Based Meals Delivered. MamaSezz. Retrieved July 18, 2022, from https://www.mamasezz.com/blogs/recipes/cooking-with-caroline- creamy-plant-based-avocado-pasta

Chapter 2

1. Mayo Clinic Staff. (n.d.). Exercise: 7 benefits of regular physical activity. Mayo Clinic. Retrieved July 18, 2022, from https://www.mayoclinic.org/healthy-lifestyle/fitness/in-depth/exercise/art-2004839

2. Watson, S. (2021, February 14). How Exercise Can Help With Adult ADHD: Brain Chemistry and More. WebMD. Retrieved July 19, 2022, from https://www.webmd.com/add-adhd/adult-adhd-and-exercise

3. Baek, S. S. (2014, Dec 31). Effect of exercise on hyperactivity, impulsivity and dopamine D2 receptor

expression in the substantia nigra and striatum of spontaneous hypertensive rats. NCBI. Retrieved July 19, 2022, from https://www.ncbi.nlm.nih.-gov/pmc/articles/PMC4322029/

4. Lynch, B. (2017, September 8). Exercise may give us more impulse control. Futurity. Retrieved July 29, 2022, from https://www.futurity.org/exercise- self-control-1 37492/

5. Diamond, A. (201 , January 19). Effects of Physical Exercise on Executive Functions: Going beyond Simply Moving to Moving with Thought. NCBI. Retrieved July 19, 2022, from https://www.ncbi.nlm.nih.gov/pmc/articles/PMC4437637/

6. Williams, V. (2022, February 4). How Exercises Benefits the Brain. US News Health. Retrieved July 18, 2022, from https://health.usnews.com/health-care/for-better/articles/how-exercise-benefits-brain-health

7. Choi, J. W., Han, D. H., Kang, K. D., Jung, H. Y., & Renshaw, P. F. (201). Aerobic exercise and attention deficit hyperactivity disorder: brain research. Medicine and science in sports and exercise, 47(1), 33–39. https://doi.org/10.1249/MSS.0000000000000373

8. Reynolds, G. (2019, July 24). How Weight Training Changes the Brain. The New York Times. Retrieved August 2, 2022, from https://www.nytimes.-com/2019/07/24/well/move/how-weight-training-changes-the- brain.html

9. Strength training can help protect the brain from degeneration. (2020, February 11). The University of Sydney. Retrieved July 29, 2022, from https://www.sydney.edu.au/news-

opinion/news/2020/02/11/strength-training-can-help-protect-the-brain-from-degeneration.html

10. Corliss, J. (2021, December 1). High-intensity exercise and your heart. Harvard Health. Retrieved July 23, 2022, from https://www.health.har-vard.edu/exercise-and-fitness/high-intensity-exercise-and-your-heart

Chapter 3

1. Wajszilber, D., Santiseban, J. A., & Gruber, R. (2018). Sleep disorders in patients with ADHD: impact and management challenges. Nature and science of sleep, 10, 4 3–480. https://doi.org/10.2147/NSS.S163074

2. Lunsford-Avery, J. R., & Kollins, S. H. (2018, September 3). Delayed Circa- dian Rhythm Phase: A Cause of Late-Onset ADHD among Adolescents? NCBI. Retrieved July 22, 2022, from https://www.ncbi.nlm.nih.-gov/pmc/articles/PMC6487490/

3. LeGates, T. A., Fernandez, D. C., & Hattar, S. (2014). Light as a central modulator of circadian rhythms, sleep and affect. Nature reviews. Neuro- science, 1 (7), 443–4 4. https://doi.org/10.1038/nrn3743

4. Olivardia, R. (2022, March 31). ADD and Sleep Apnea: How Sleep Issues Can Look Like ADHD. ADDitude. Retrieved August 2, 2022, from https://www.additudemag.com/add-and-sleep-apnea-problems-solutions/

Chapter 4

1. Miller, G. (2021, Sept 30). Meeting Your Goals When You Have ADHD: 9 Helpful Tips. Psych Central. Retrieved July 20, 2022, from https://psych-central.com/adhd/meeting-your-goals-when-you-have-adhd#types-of- goals
2. Rapson, S. (2021, November 2). ADHD Goal Setting. Unconventional Organisation. Retrieved July 20, 2022, from https://www.unconventionalorganisa-tion.com/post/adhd-goal-setting
3. SAMHSA. (n.d.). Setting Goals and Developing Specific, Measurable, Achievable, Relevant, and Time-bound Objectives. SAMHSA. Retrieved July 28, 2022, from https://www.samhsa.gov/sites/de-fault/files/nc-smart- goals-fact-sheet.pdf
4. Honos, L. (2022, June 1). Achieving Personal Goals with ADHD: 6 Super Skills. ADDitude. Retrieved July 20, 2022, from https://www.additudemag.-com/achieving-personal-goals-adhd/

Chapter 5

1. Curb, W. (2021, September 13). How to Plan Your Day — Hacking Your ADHD. Hacking Your ADHD. Retrieved July 30, 2022, from https://www.hackingy-ouradhd.com/podcast/how-to-plan-your-day
2. Time Management and ADHD: Day Planners. (n.d.). CHADD. Retrieved July 30, 2022, from https://chadd.org/for-adults/time-management-planner/

Chapter 6

1. The ACTIVATE (TM) Physical Exercise Program |
   Improve Cognitive Skills. (2020, June 30). C8
   Sciences. Retrieved August 5 , 2022, from
   https://www.c8sciences.com/adhd-and-structured-
   environment-class- room-tips/
2. Hurley, K. (2020, January 10). ADHD in The
   Workplace - Tips To Flourish In The Work
   Environment. Psycom.net. Retrieved August 2, 2022,
   from https://www.psycom.net/adhd-in-the-workplace/
3. Betker, C. (2017, November 17). Environmental
   Strategies for Managing Attention Deficit
   Hyperactivity Disorder | Insight Medical Publishing.
   Journal of Childhood & Developmental Disorders.
   Retrieved August 13, 2022, from https://childhood-
   developmental-disorders.imedpub.com/en-
   vironmental-strategis-for-managing-attention-deficit-
   hyperactivity- disorder.php?aid=2106
4. Maynard, S. (2022, March 11). Making Peace With
   Your Clutter: A Guide for ADHD Adults. ADDitude.
   Retrieved August 2, 2022, from https://www.addi-
   tudemag.com/making-peace-with-your-clutter/
5. ADHD and Organizing Your Space. (2020, March 3).
   Dr. Hallowell. Retrieved August 2, 2022, from
   https://drhallowell.com/2020/03/03/adhd- and-
   organizing-your-space/

Chapter 7

1. Benefits of Deep Breathing. (2014, November 3).
   Urban Balance. Retrieved August 4, 2022, from
   https://www.urbanbalance.com/benefits-deep-
   breathing/

2. DiLonardo, M. J. (2021, July 3). Deep Breathing: Step-by-Step Stress Relief. WebMD. Retrieved August 4, 2022, from https://www.web-md.com/parent- ing/how-to-deep-breathe

3. Shepard, M. (n.d.). Meditating With ADHD: Tips, Strategies, Resources. Verywell Mind. Retrieved August 4, 2022, from https://www.verywell-mind.com/best-meditation-strategies-for-people-with-adhd- 201908 (*How to Meditate Effectively — Even With ADHD*, n.d.) 168

4. Spend Time Outside to Improve ADHD Symptoms. (2017, June 22). CHADD. Retrieved August 4, 2022, from https://chadd.org/adhd-week- ly/spend-time-outside-to-improve-adhd-symptoms

5. Fitzgerald, S. (2019, October 18). Forest bathing: what it is and where to do it. National Geographic. Retrieved August 4, 2022, from https://www.na-tionalgeographic.com/travel/article/forest-bathing-nature-walk-health

6. Li, Q. (2018, May 1). The Benefits of 'Forest Bathing'. TIME. Retrieved August 4, 2022, from https://time.com/ 2 9602/japanese-forest-bathing/

Chapter 9

1. Levine, H. (2022, January 17). How Mindful Meditation and Yoga Can Help Treat ADHD. WebMD. Retrieved August 11, 2022, from https://www.webmd.com/add-adhd/adhd-mindful ness-meditation-yoga

2. Taylor VA, Daneault V, Grant J, Scavone G, Breton E, Roffe-Vidal S, Beauregard M. Impact of meditation training on the default mode network during a restful state. *Social Cognitive & Affective Neuroscience.* 2013;8(1):4–14. doi:

10.1093/scan/nsr087. Retrieved August 11, 2022, from https://www.ncbi.nlm.nih.gov/pmc/articles/PMC4403871/#R114

Chapter 10

1. White, H. (2019, March 5). The Creativity of ADHD. Scientific American. Retrieved August 12, 2022, from https://www.scientificamerican.-com/article/the-creativity-of-adhd/
2. White, H. (2019, March 5). The Creativity of ADHD. Scientific American. Retrieved August 12, 2022, from https://www.scientificamerican.com/article/the-creativity-of-adhd/

Bibliography

The ACTIVATE (TM) *Physical Exercise Program | Improve Cognitive Skills.* (2020, June 30). C8 Sciences. Retrieved August 5 , 2022, from https://www.c8sciences.- com/adhd-and-structured-environment-classroom-tips/

ADHD and Organizing Your Space. (2020, March 3). Dr. Hallowell. Retrieved August 2, 2022, from https://drhallowell.com/2020/03/03/adhd-and-orga-nizing-your-space/

ADHD Diet Plan: Foods to Eat & Avoid to Help ADD Symptoms. (n.d.). ADDi-tude. Retrieved July 15, 2022, from https://www.additudemag.com/adhd-diet- nutrition-sugar/

ADHD Diet Plan: Foods to Eat & Avoid to Help ADD Symptoms. (n.d.). ADDi-tude. Retrieved August 4, 2022, from https://www.additudemag.com/adhd-diet- nutrition-sugar

Aerobic Exercise and Attention Deficit Hyperactivity Disorder: Brain Research. (n.d.). NCBI. Retrieved August 2, 2022, from https://www.ncbi.nlm.nih.-gov/pmc/articles/PMC 04911/

Baek, S. S. (2014, Dec 31). *Effect of exercise on hyperactivity, impulsivity and dopamine D2 receptor expression in the substantia nigra and striatum of spontaneous hypertensive rats.* NCBI. Retrieved July 19, 2022, from https://www.ncbi.nlm.nih.gov/pmc/articles/PMC4322029/

Benefits of Deep Breathing. (2014, November 3). Urban Balance. Retrieved August 4, 2022, from https://www.urbanbalance.com/benefits-deep-breathing/

Betker, C. (2017, November 17). *Environmental Strategies for Managing Attention Deficit Hyperactivity Disorder | Insight Medical Publishing.* Journal of Childhood & Developmental Disorders. Retrieved August 13, 2022, from https://child- hood-developmental-disorders.imedpub.com/envi-ronmental-strategies-for- managing-attention-deficit-hyperactivity-disor-der.php?aid=2106

Breus, M. (2022, June 22). *ADHD and Sleep.* The Sleep Doctor. Retrieved July 20, 2022, from https://thesleepdoctor.com/mental-health/adhd-and-sleep/

Carlson, L. (2017, June 22). *Is your brain on fire? Symptoms of brain inflam-mation | ChiroPro Performance Center.* | ChiroPro Performance Center. Retrieved July 1 , 2022, from https://chiroproperformance.com/is-your-brain-on-fire- symptoms-of-brain-inflammation/

Bibliography

Carlson, L. (2017, June 22). *Is your brain on fire? Symptoms of brain inflammation | ChiroPro Performance Center.* | ChiroPro Performance Center. Retrieved August 4, 2022, from https://chiroproperformance.com/is-your-brain-on- fire-symptoms-of-brain-inflammation/

Corliss, J. (2021, December 1). *High-intensity exercise and your heart.* Harvard Health. Retrieved July 23, 2022, from https://www.health.harvard.edu/exercise-and-fitness/high-intensity-exercise-and-your-heart

Curb, W. (2021, September 13). *How to Plan Your Day — Hacking Your ADHD.* Hacking Your ADHD. Retrieved July 30, 2022, from https://www.hackingy- ouradhd.com/podcast/how-to-plan-your-day

Diamond, A. (201 , January 19). *Effects of Physical Exercise on Executive Functions: Going beyond Simply Moving to Moving with Thought.* NCBI. Retrieved July 19, 2022, from https://www.ncbi.nlm.nih.gov/pmc/articles/PMC4437637/

DiLonardo, M. J. (2021, July 3). *Deep Breathing: Step-by-Step Stress Relief.* WebMD. Retrieved August 4, 2022, from https://www.webmd.com/parenting/how-to-deep-breathe

Easy Vegan Breakfast Hash with Veggies and Beans. (2021, March 12). Karissa's Vegan Kitchen. Retrieved July 18, 2022, from https://www.karissasvegankitchen.com/bean-potato-veggie-breakfast-hash/

Environmental Strategies for Managing Attention Deficit Hyperactivity Disorder | Insight Medical Publishing. (n.d.). Journal of Childhood & Developmental Disorders. Retrieved August 2, 2022, from https://childhood-developmen- tal-disorders.imedpub.com/environmental-strategies-for-managing-atten- tion-deficit-hyperactivity-disorder.php?aid=2106

Executive Function & Self-Regulation. (n.d.). Center on the Developing Child at Harvard University. Retrieved July 22, 2022, from https://developingchild.harvard.edu/science/key-concepts/executive-function/

Fawley, C. D. (n.d.). *Creamy Plant-Based Avocado Pasta Recipe | MamaSezz Plant Based Meals Delivered.* MamaSezz. Retrieved July 18, 2022, from https://www.mamasezz.com/blogs/recipes/cooking-with-caroline-creamy-plant-based-avocado-pasta

Fawley, C. D. (n.d.). *Vegan Curried Chickpea Salad Recipe | MamaSezz Plant Based Prepared Meals.* MamaSezz. Retrieved July 27, 2022, from https://www.ma- masezz.com/blogs/recipes/curried-chickpea-salad-recipe

Fitzgerald, S. (2019, October 18). *Forest bathing: what it is and where to do it.* National Geographic. Retrieved August 4, 2022, from https://www.nationalgeographic.com/travel/article/forest-bathing-nature-walk-health

Hallowell, E. (2021, January 12). *Undiagnosed Adult ADHD or ADD: Why Diagnosis Can Save a Life.* ADDitude. Retrieved July 7, 2022, from https://www.addi-   tudemag.com/undiagnosed-adult-adhd-diagnosis-symptoms/

Honos, L. (2022, June 1). *Achieving Personal Goals with ADHD: 6 Super Skills*. ADDitude. Retrieved July 20, 2022, from https://www.additudemag.-com/achieving-personal-goals-adhd/

How to Meditate Effectively — Even with ADHD. (n.d.). ADDitude. Retrieved August 4, 2022, from https://www.additudemag.com/how-to-meditate-for-adhd-symptoms/

Hurley, K. (2020, January 10). *ADHD in The Workplace - Tips To Flourish In The Work Environment*. Psycom.net. Retrieved August 2, 2022, from https://www.psycom.net/adhd-in-the-workplace/

Legg, T. J. (2019, September 18). *ADHD and Alcohol: How They're Linked Plus Interactions & Risk Factors*. Healthline. Retrieved July 19, 2022, from https://www.healthline.com/health/adhd-and-alcohol#risk-factors

Levine, H. (2022, January 17). *How Mindful Meditation and Yoga Can Help Treat ADHD*. WebMD. Retrieved August 11, 2022, from https://www.web-md.- com/add-adhd/adhd-mindfulness-meditation-yoga

Li, Q. (2018, May 1). *The Benefits of 'Forest Bathing'*. TIME. Retrieved August 4, 2022, from https://time.com/ 2 9602/japanese-forest-bathing/

Lunsford-Avery, J. R., & Kollins, S. H. (2018, September 3). *Delayed Circadian Rhythm Phase: A Cause of Late-Onset ADHD among Adolescents?* NCBI. Retrieved July 22, 2022, from https://www.ncbi.nlm.nih.gov/pmc/articles/PMC6487490/

Lynch, B. (2017, September 8). *Exercise may give us more impulse control*. Futurity. Retrieved July 29, 2022, from https://www.futurity.org/exercise-self- control-1 37492/

Maynard, S. (2022, March 11). *Making Peace With Your Clutter: A Guide for ADHD Adults*. ADDitude. Retrieved August 2, 2022, from https://www.addi- tudemag.com/making-peace-with-your-clutter/

Mayo Clinic Staff. (n.d.). *Exercise: 7 benefits of regular physical activity*. Mayo Clinic. Retrieved July 18, 2022, from https://www.mayoclin-ic.org/healthy- lifestyle/fitness/in-depth/exercise/art-20048389

Meda, K. (2019, November 26). *How to Manipulate Brain Waves for a Better Mental State*. The Nexus. Retrieved July 28, 2022, from https://nexus.jeffer-son.e-   du/science-and-technology/how-to-manipulate-brain-waves-for-a-better- mental-state/

Miller, G. (2021, Sept 30). *Meeting Your Goals When You Have ADHD: 9 Helpful Tips*. Psych Central. Retrieved July 20, 2022, from https://psychcen-tral.- com/adhd/meeting-your-goals-when-you-have-adhd#types-of- goals

Newmark, S. (n.d.). *The ADHD Diet Plan: Healthy Foods and Supplements for*

Kids & Adults. ADDitude. Retrieved August 4, 2022, from https://www.addi- tudemag.com/adhd-diet-for-kids-food-fix/

Olivardia, R. (2022, March 31). *ADD and Sleep Apnea: How Sleep Issues Can Look Like ADHD.* ADDitude. Retrieved August 2, 2022, from https://www.addi- tudemag.com/add-and-sleep-apnea-problems-solutions/

Omega-3 Benefits to ADHD Brains: Fish Oil for Focus. (2021, May 5). ADDitude. Retrieved August 4, 2022, from https://www.additudemag.com/adhd-omega-3-benefits

Pacheco, D. (2022, March 11). *The Best Temperature for Sleep: Advice & Tips.* Sleep Foundation. Retrieved July 23, 2022, from https://www.sleepfoundation.org/bedroom-environment/best-temperature-for-sleep

Pandolfo, P., Machado, N., Köfalvi, A., Takahashi, R. N., & Cunha, R. A. (2013). Caffeine regulates frontocorticostriatal dopamine transporter density and improves attention and cognitive deficits in an animal model of attention deficit hyperactivity disorder,. *European Neuropsychopharmacology,, 23*(4), 317-328. https://doi.org/10.1016/j.euroneuro.2012.04.011.

Rapson, S. (2021, November 2). *ADHD Goal Setting.* Unconventional Organisa- tion. Retrieved July 20, 2022, from https://www.unconventionalorganisation.com/post/adhd-goal-setting

Reynolds, G. (2019, July 24). *How Weight Training Changes the Brain.* The New York Times. Retrieved August 2, 2022, from https://www.nytimes.com/2019/07/24/well/move/how-weight-training-changes-the-brain.html

SAMHSA. (n.d.). *Setting Goals and Developing Specific, Measurable, Achievable, Rele vant, and Time-bound Objectives.* SAMHSA. Retrieved July 28, 2022, from https://www.samhsa.gov/sites/default/files/nc-smart-goals-fact-sheet.pdf Shepard, M. (n.d.). *Meditating With ADHD: Tips, Strategies, Resources.* Verywell Mind. Retrieved August 4, 2022, from https://www.verywellmind.com/best-meditation-strategies-for-people-with-adhd- 201908

Spend Time Outside to Improve ADHD Symptoms. (2017, June 22). CHADD.Retrieved August 4, 2022, from https://chadd.org/adhd-weekly/spend-time-outside-to-improve-adhd-symptoms

Strength training can help protect the brain from degeneration. (2020, February 11). The University of Sydney. Retrieved July 29, 2022, from https://www.syd- ney.edu.au/news-opinion/news/2020/02/11/strength-training-can-help- protect-the-brain-from-degeneration.html

Thompson, J. (2022, January 14). *Alpha state of mind.* Atlassian. Retrieved July 28, 2022, from https://www.atlassian.com/blog/productivity/alpha-brain- waves-are-associated-with-a-flow-state-of-mind-heres-how-to-ride-yours

Time Management and ADHD: Day Planners. (n.d.). CHADD. Retrieved July 30, 2022, from https://chadd.org/for-adults/time-management-planner/

Vath, C. (n.d.). *Caffeine and ADHD: Is This Natural Treatment Safe & Effective?* ADDitude. Retrieved August 4, 2022, from https://www.additudemag.- com/adhd-caffeine-treatment/

Watson, S. (2021, February 14). *How Exercise Can Help With Adult ADHD: Brain Chemistry and More*. WebMD. Retrieved July 19, 2022, from https://www.webmd.com/add-adhd/adult-adhd-and-exercise

White, H. (2019, March 5). *The Creativity of ADHD*. Scientific American. Retrieved August 12, 2022, from https://www.scientificamerican.com/article/the-creativity-of-adhd/

Whole-Foods, Plant-Based Diet: A Detailed Beginner's Guide. (2018, June 12). Healthline. Retrieved August 4, 2022, from https://www.healthline.com/nutrition/plant-based-diet-guide

Williams, V. (2022, February 4). *How Exercises Benefits the Brain*. US News Health. Retrieved July 18, 2022, from https://health.usnews.com/health-care/for-better/articles/how-exercise-benefits-brain-health

Afterword

I dearly hope some of these strategies can help you. If this book has inspired you to turn those negative ADHD labels into your very own superpowers, kindly consider writing a review on Amazon.
Maybe others, in the same position as you, may find this information and get the push they need to thrive with ADHD as well.

~

Deep gratitude!
~Yvette Quintana

About the Author

~

M. Yvette Quintana is an entrepreneur, writer/publisher and outdoor adventure guide. She has lived with ADHD most of her life, although she didn't get properly diagnosed until later. At one time she had five part-time jobs, not out of necessity. She has managed her abundant energy and behavior through a healthy lifestyle and mindful training that has brought balance and clarity to her own life.

Quintana wants to help others find healthy and appropriate ways to manage ADHD and make positive changes that may greatly impact the quality of their lives.

～

"She needed a hero, so that's what she became."
~Anonymous

Made in the USA
Middletown, DE
03 September 2023